Cambridge Elements ≡

Elements in the Global Middle Ages
edited by
Geraldine Heng
University of Texas at Austin
Susan Noakes
University of Minnesota, Twin Cities

SLAVERY IN EAST ASIA

Don J. Wyatt
Middlebury College

Shaftesbury Road, Cambridge CB2 8EA, United Kingdom

One Liberty Plaza, 20th Floor, New York, NY 10006, USA

477 Williamstown Road, Port Melbourne, VIC 3207, Australia

314–321, 3rd Floor, Plot 3, Splendor Forum, Jasola District Centre,
New Delhi – 110025, India

103 Penang Road, #05–06/07, Visioncrest Commercial, Singapore 238467

Cambridge University Press is part of Cambridge University Press & Assessment,
a department of the University of Cambridge.

We share the University's mission to contribute to society through the pursuit of
education, learning and research at the highest international levels of excellence.

www.cambridge.org
Information on this title: www.cambridge.org/9781009001700

DOI: 10.1017/9781009007009

First published 2022

A catalogue record for this publication is available from the British Library.

ISBN 978-1-009-00170-0 Paperback
ISSN 2632-3427 (online)
ISSN 2632-3419 (print)

Slavery in East Asia

Elements in the Global Middle Ages

DOI: 10.1017/9781009007009
First published online: December 2022

Don J. Wyatt
Middlebury College

Author for correspondence: Don J. Wyatt, wyatt@middlebury.edu

Abstract: In premodern China, Korea, Japan, and Vietnam, just as in the far less culturally cohesive countries composing the West of the Middle Ages, enslavement was an assumed condition of servitude warranting little examination, as the power and profits it afforded to the slaver made it a convention pursued unreflectively. Slavery in medieval East Asia shared with the West the commonplace assumption that nearly all humans were potential chattel, that once they had become owned beings, they could then be either sold or inherited. Yet, despite being representative of perhaps the most universalizable human practice of that age, slavery in medieval East Asia was also endowed with its own distinctive traits and traditions. Our awareness of these features of distinction contributes immeasurably to a more nuanced understanding of slavery as the ubiquitous and openly practiced institution that it once was and the now illicit and surreptitious one that it intractably remains.

This Element also has a video abstract: www.cambridge.org/slaveryineastasia

Keywords: slavery, bondage, human trafficking, East Asia, Middle Ages

ISBNs: 9781009001700 (PB), 9781009007009 (OC)
ISSNs: 2632-3427 (online), 2632-3419 (print)

Contents

Preface

This Element represents a distillation of much of my previous and ongoing research on institutionalized slavery, which, while heretofore confined to the premodern Chinese context, has expanded both regionally and comparatively to embrace more broadly its socio-institutional history amidst its East Asian parameters overall. As demonstrated by what follows, during what were mutually overlapping and intersecting periods that are discretely regarded as having been "medieval," Chinese conventions in slavery profoundly and impactfully influenced those that became practiced in the surrounding cultures of Korea, Japan, and Vietnam. However, just as in other areas of sociocultural activity, whether at that time or later, in the matter of slavery, the imprint of the Chinese model on these neighboring entities and their polities never succeeded in being overweeningly determinative. Despite the many interconnections that existed among them, we will come to appreciate as much or more how as well as why medieval China, Korea, Japan, and Vietnam each came to exhibit its own irreducibly unique characteristics with respect to practices in enslavement.

Medieval East Asian Slavery in Overview

Let us begin our deliberations in earnest by observing that for several millennia before the Common Era years of approximately 500 to 1500, the four principal cultural constituents of the East Asian region, China, Korea, Japan, and Vietnam,[1] to greatly varying extents, all evinced entrenched and self-perpetuating systems of slavery, bondage, and the trafficking of enslaved individuals. Therefore, just as is true for other regions of the world where it flourished during the same span of about ten centuries – so often, from the Western viewpoint, referred to as the "medieval" age or age of "late antiquity" – that is our epoch of focus, we should regard the slaving systems that were then operative throughout East Asia as being fully mature ones that had prehistoric roots. Indeed, as is effectively the case for anywhere else in which the phenomenon occurred, any inquiry into the prehistory of East Asian civilization itself is pursued only imperfectly if undertaken without reference to slavery and its attendant, typically also violent, practices.

In the case of China, an abundance of continually emerging archaeological evidence attests to the embeddedness of inherited practices of enslavement in the most remote past. We find such to be the case because of the close connection with or even primal essentialness of slavery in a truly ancient tradition of human sacrifice – one that is generally regarded by most authorities as having the longest history in the world, spanning from Chinese Neolithic times

---

[1] For more on the rationale based on Sinism for the inclusion of medieval Vietnam as properly a constituent of the East Asian cultural zone, see Kang, 2010 [repr. 2012]: 25–49.

(ca. 8500–ca. 1500 BCE) until the twentieth century (Yates, 2013: 158). Indeed, as Hilda Hookham graphically described, slaves seem to have been an assumed inclusion of all royal funerary rites:

> In some cases slaves appear to have been buried alive, as in the mausoleum of an aristocratic family unearthed in Anyang County, where seventy living people were buried with the dead. In other cases headless skeletons have been found in sets of ten. The heads, also in decimal sets, have been discovered elsewhere. Living slaves were often tethered at the neck to prevent flight from their work; their hands were chained at night. (Hookham, 1970: 2)

Consequently, among the social phenomena on which the ceaseless excavation of the burial sites of earliest Chinese nobility continues to cast newly informing light is surely slavery. Indisputably, the mental outlook of the slavers of this antediluvian age regarding their captives is far from fully recoverable for us. Nevertheless, one cannot help but think that the views of historian Rhoads Murphey were hardly much amiss when, specifically of the Shang (also called Yin) dynasty (ca. 1600–1045 BCE), he opined, "Slaves were not thought to have souls or spirits and thus could safely be killed; the Shang aristocrats seem not to have thought about what might happen to them if they became war captives themselves" (Murphey, 1996 [repr. 1997]: 34; Lai, 2015: 43–46, 186). At any rate, we can be certain that these particular individuals found in the tombs along with the noble interred by no means attained the level of status of any of the "companions of the dead" (*xunren* 殉人), who have been discovered at least skeletally intact and, in many instances, seem to have been given full funerary rites, as attested by having coffins and grave effects of their own (Lai, 2015: 105, 107).

In contrast to the Chinese situation, in addition to it not being of even remotely comparable vintage, there is simply far less archaeological evidence of the mortuary practices of the ancient elites of Korea, Japan, and Vietnam that has to date, at least, been either unearthed or examined. In its absence, our assertion of an inheritance of long-established slaving practices from the most ancient of times for any of these cultures, despite remaining likely in theory, remains far more a matter of speculation. However, expressly for the subsequent period of a near-millennium under our direct consideration, we are in luck because, in each instance, whether medieval China, assuredly, but also Korea, Japan, or Vietnam, the culture we scrutinize either already was or was becoming a literate one. As a result, each has left behind at least some primary source materials addressing the interwoven phenomena of slavery, bondage, and human trafficking.[2] Therefore,

---

[2] Prior to the development of what have emerged as their separate national writing systems, this initial and shared language of literacy was invariably what is now called literary or classical Chinese. See Henthorn, 1971 (repr. 1974): 145–46; Hane, 1991: 25, 26, 49; Kiernan, 2017 (repr. 2019): 125–27.

in the case of premodern China, our success in investigating these activities will depend largely on our capacity for interpreting the sizable corpus of preserved evidentiary sources that, in bearing directly on these subjects, complements the archaeological one. By contrast, in the cases of premodern Korea, Japan, and Vietnam, whatever insight we can garner on the same activities will hinge on our capacity to identify and exploit three far less copious corpora of much more diffuse materials dealing with these same activities.

Despite the venerable antiquity of at least one of its cultural components, with that of course being China, East Asia arguably coalesced in the form of a discrete and distinctly coherent regional unit only relatively late in historical terms. Most authorities agree that it is only from as recently as about the beginning of the third century CE, which is regarded as the dawning of "middle antiquity" at least from an accepted Western periodization standpoint, that we may interpret a coherent East Asian region as having first emerged (Holcombe, 2011: 3–5). To be sure, among the representative civilizations comprising what we today regard as the constitutive cultural pillars of the East Asian region, none has asserted dominance over greater span of its duration than that of China. Moreover, for the period from roughly the sixth to the sixteenth century that serves as our targeted temporal locus of inquiry, China was more culturally dominant over the East Asian region as a cultural zone than it had ever previously been. Consequently, in acknowledgment of its centrality to the knowledge thus far accrued concerning slavery, bondage, and human trafficking as the practices occurred within the East Asian context, the Chinese paradigm deservedly serves as the cynosure, necessarily constituting the prime reference point for the deliberations that ensue in this study.

However, even as the Chinese example is utilized throughout as chief paradigm and touchstone, we will unavoidably encounter and be tasked with accounting for aspects of Korean, Japanese, and Vietnamese distinctiveness with respect to the subject of enslavement. We will find that the circumstances of human bondage as they existed throughout the medieval East Asian world will manifest variability while they simultaneously evince coherence, with the former oftentimes enriching our understanding in ways the latter cannot. For example, in Korea, we will see that, upon its establishment at the close of the Goryeo (or Koryŏ) dynasty (918–1392) and beginning of the Joseon (also Chosŏn or sometimes Yi) dynasty (1392–1897/1910), the Korean system of slavery, because of its legal strictures mandating slave status as hereditary, came to represent what the eminent sociologist of comparative slaveries Orlando Patterson has called the East Asian region's "most advanced system of slavery" (Patterson, 1982: 143).

Contrastingly, albeit extensive, particularly for the period of our coverage, we will find that the putative incidences of the practice of slavery, bondage, and/or human trafficking may only be assessed with considerable caution and amidst a host of qualifications in connection with Japan. We find, for example, that the Indigenous Ainu tribes of Japan are reported as having been notorious for selling their own relatives and wards as well as their unwanted wives and children into slavery, not out of obvious economic exigency, as was often commonplace in the turbulent, war-torn eras prior to the unification of 1600, but purely for reasons of profit. However, we must be wary of such pronouncements, not merely because they tend to constitute anachronistic imputations, as opposed to retrospective interpolations, of much later ages but also because they are likely more reflective than not of the self-serving propagandist rhetoric of the dominating slave-purchasing and slave-trading elements of what then constituted Japanese society than dispassionate readings of the behavior of the Ainu themselves (Schrenck, 1858: III, 646; Patterson, 1982: 131). Indeed, just the extreme dearth of sources available for the discernment of slaving practices in Japan, at least prior to the exploitation of those practices by Europeans – and chiefly by the Portuguese – at the beginning in the sixteenth century, poses a serious impediment to our understanding.

In medieval Vietnam, from the Đại Cồ Việt period of rule at Hoa Lư (965–1005) through the Lý dynasty (1009–1225) to the establishment of the Trần dynasty (1225–1413), although it became increasingly nativized, slavery was largely the condition of servitude imposed on contiguously abiding regional outsiders, usually as captives of war. Frequently so enslaved were members of the Chams of Champa, inhabitants of the southeastern coastline of what is now southern Vietnam. We know little of the prevailing conditions for these earliest of the medieval slaves and even less of those endured by their precursors. However, we learn from the historian K. W. Taylor that, over the course of time, the sources of slaves in Vietnam diversified, that they "could be peasants who sold themselves into slavery to improve their lives, or prisoners of war, or people from other lands brought by merchants" and that these slaves "served many functions from manual laborers to skilled craftspeople" (Taylor, 2013: 122). Nevertheless, these challenges we confront with the Korean, Japanese, and Vietnamese cases notwithstanding, inasmuch as any premodern mode of East Asian slavery, bondage, and human trafficking ever existed, we must endeavor to comprehend it by taking into account not only the developmental experience of China but also those of Korea, Japan, and Vietnam as fully as we can.

Medieval East Asian Slavery Defined and Ideologized

Universal consensus on a definition for slavery may well forever elude us.[3] However, within the premodern Chinese – and, by extension, premodern East Asian – context, the slave was, by definition, a person who had been deprived of all liberty and thus was subject to being either bought, or sold, or gifted. Moreover, such persons so subjected became classified by a universalized and eventually legally codified set of terms. What eventually emerged as by far the most common term for such people was *nubi* 奴婢 (literally, "male and female slaves"; Korean, *nobi*; Japanese, *nuhi*; Vietnamese, *người hầu*).[4]

Yet, specifically in relation to China as well as the East Asian context generally, just as important to our understanding of the human being as having been reduced to this state of servitude by the terms by which they were referred to is for us to recognize what were, on the whole, the fundamentally punitive origins of slavery itself. From the very first, in China, to be sure, slave status was customarily viewed as a condition that befell those who had either contravened or undermined or otherwise resisted authority. Hence, enslavement was foremost thought to be a penalty for aberrant or refractory behavior and, whether consciously or not, the association of it with criminality and, by extension, the penal system always remained quite intimate (Patterson, 1982: 43, 44).

This punitive genesis of slavery in China is further illustrated by the fact that, from what is likely time immemorial on down to modern times, the Chinese – or, retrospectively, even those earliest direct ancestors of them who would eventually constitute the dominant Han ethnic majority – have practiced endogenous *as well as* exogenous slavery. In other words, with no less apparent readiness and frequency than they have enslaved outsiders, the Chinese have also historically enslaved members of their own majority ethnic Han kind, with the precipitating cause almost invariantly having been the commission of some order of infraction against prevailing authority. Moreover, a consideration of the dissimilar paths that might lead to the punishment with enslavement of the members of these two disparate groups is also illuminating.

From the time of the Shang dynasty until well into the two-plus millennia era following the imperial unification in 221 BCE, the archetypal enslaved outsider was certainly the enemy combatant of either a resistant or rebellious non-Chinese tribe captured as a prisoner of war. Availing ourselves of the interpretive theory of social death postulated by Orlando Patterson, we may deem such enslavement of this individual to have been representative of slavery in its

---

[3] See the provocative discussion of the challenges in Miers, 2004: 1–15.

[4] For more on the original Chinese interpretation and its nuances, see Pulleyblank, 1958: 193, 203, 205–6, 208, 214).

intrusive conception, whereby the victim was the "foreigner, enemy, and infidel, fit only for enslavement" (Patterson, 1982: 41), forcibly extirpated from his homeland and inserted as lifelong captive into the environs of his masters. By contrast, the paradigmatic insider who became subject to enslavement in premodern China was someone of respectable or even elite status whose perhaps single adverse action had suddenly precipitated societal expulsion. In the most conspicuous instances, this infraction was seditious and whereas death was invariably the penalty exacted on the actual perpetrator of a capital offense, enslavement was collaterally imposed on all of his surviving kin. Patterson refers to this conception of enslavement as *extrusive*, wherein those who once belonged become expelled, ostracized, and relegated to outsider status through bondage, and Patterson furthermore astutely concludes that, among the traditional Chinese, "penal enslavement was the foremost source of slaves" (Patterson, 1982: 127).

In Korea, the definition of what constituted a slave was roughly comparable to that which had long obtained in China, especially given the similarly punitive function as an impetus for the origin of slavery there (Salem, 1978: 4–6, 155). Yet, even while more fixed as immutable for life, we also find that being enslaved in Korea denoted a status that was more fluid, and also layered with moral connotations that were absent in the Chinese case, all very possibly because of the almost exclusively endogenous character of Korean slavery. Having existed since a time prior to the pre-unification Three Kingdoms era (57 BCE–668 CE),[5] when the Chinese paradigm of "good" versus "base" people was adopted, at least in the longest-enduring state of Silla 신라 (Chinese, Xinluo 新羅) (Seth, 2016: 62),[6] slaves in Korea were persons from whom, according to the Confucian outlook also adopted from China perhaps as early as the first century BCE, Heaven was thought to have withdrawn its favor. Also in Korea, in accordance with Confucianism, a hierarchical relationship between master and slave, mirroring the idealized one espoused between ruler and subject or father and son, developed. The *nobi*, viewed as appendages, were even eventually propagandized via Confucian dictates as being extensions of the very bodies of their masters (Lovins, 2022: 178–79), all toward the purpose of course of justifying the necessity of their enslavement.

---

[5] To be distinguished from the post-unification period of the same name that spanned only from the year 220 to 284 of the Common Era in China.

[6] Silla (also called Shilla) existed from 57 BCE to 935 CE. Its companion kingdoms, which it conquered in succession, were Baekje 백제 (Chinese, Baiji 百濟), also called Nambuyeo 남부여 (Chinese, Nanfuyu 南扶餘), which existed from 18 BCE to 660 CE, and Goguryeo (also written Koguryŏ) 고구려 (Chinese, Gaojuli 高句麗), which existed from 37 BCE to 668 CE.

So pervasive did slavery become in medieval Korea that, by the time of the onset of the Joseon period at the close of the fourteenth century, Korean slaves had become socially indistinct from freemen, even though this diverse latter group in which they were included was wholly distinct from the ruling class itself. Many *nobi* possessed property and civil rights and held legal entities. Consequently, some scholars have argued for the inappropriateness of referring to the *nobi* as slaves, likening them instead to European-style serfs (Kim, 2004: 153, 154, 155, 156, 157; Miers, 2004: 7, 10–11). Whether tenable or not, this dissenting opinion is in fact reinforced by at least two key factors. First, the Korean term for an actual slave in our own sense of the word is not *nobi* but instead *noye* 노예 (Chinese, *nuli* 奴隷). At least by the Joseon dynasty, the former oftentimes enjoyed property rights that, in the manner of the Western notion of serfdom, permitted some level of independence and some modicum of freedom whereas the latter simply never did. Second, uniquely within the East Asian enslavement context, some *nobi* of Korea were not only landowning but actually owned their own *nobi* (Salem Unruh, 1976: 31; Palais, 1998: 39, 50), thereby, somewhat astoundingly and counterintuitively, from the Western perspective, being slaves who themselves owned slaves.

In Japan, in contrast to Korea, owing especially to the presence of Indigenous Ainu peoples, both the endogenous and the exogenous systems of slavery, bondage, and human trafficking seem to have existed since the earliest historically verifiable times. However, we know painfully little in practical terms either about how these systems might have functioned or the levels of comprehensiveness they attained. The *Weishu* 魏書 or *Weizhi* 魏志 (*History of Wei* or *Record of Wei*), an authorized history of a kingdom in North China that endured only from 220 to 265 CE, completed in 297, does contain an entry on the exportation from Japan into China of at least one Japanese slave. However, it does not indicate which system was involved as the conduit. Nor does it convey whether such procurement was common practice at that time. It does, nonetheless, provide us with the earliest name for such slaves, or conceivably prisoners of war, who were called *shengkou* 生口 (Japanese, *seikō*; literally, "living mouths") (Chen, 1984: *Weishu* 30.855; Brown, 1993: 25).

In Vietnam, the earliest available evidence suggests that, much as in the case of China, those near-neighboring outsiders, probably distinguished primarily along cultural-linguistic lines – once defeated in war and taken alive as captives – were most susceptible to enslavement. Moreover, we find that these individuals included not only the familiar Chams to the coastal south and Khmers of what is modern-day Cambodia or Kampuchea, the former with whom there had been long-standing conflicts,[7] but also many other peoples who shared either recognized or unrecognized contiguous borders with the Vietnamese. As historian Ben Kiernan informs us, "The Lý court assigned major Buddhist temples a labor force of Cham prisoners, who worked as artisans and played a leading role in the flourishing art and architecture of Đại Việt's proliferating monasteries. Cham slaves also lived and worked in the temple of the Phù Đổng earth spirit" (Kiernan, 2017 [repr. 2019]: 154).

Additionally, during the Lý dynasty, we can assume that captives taken along what is now the northeastern Vietnamese border with Yunnan province, who were often very conceivably ethnically Han Chinese, especially if they were able-bodied and at all skilled, could of course be readily subjected to slavery. Given that Lý Đại Việt heralded the commencement of a new era when Vietnam had only very recently freed itself from Chinese dominion, perhaps the seizure of Chinese was a targeted reciprocation for the centuries of Việt women and girls having been extracted and imported into sexual servitude in China.[8] Moreover, whether they were ethnic Chinese or not, we cannot expect that all of these border-inhabiting captives of the Vietnamese met the same fate. According to Li Tana, many captured Chinese were directly impressed into service in the Vietnamese army, whereas "many others must have been resold to the foreign merchants who frequented Đại Việt, and ended up in places such as Champa" (Li, 2006: 87).

Throughout the Lý dynastic era, this non-native component of premodern Vietnamese slavery, owing to its profitability for the slavers involved, was no doubt to remain a highly identifiable component. However, paralleling the development of slavery in early medieval Japan, we learn of a perceptibly endogenous or nativist turn in medieval Vietnamese slavery. We furthermore find that this development largely coincides with the advent of the Trần dynasty in the early thirteenth century and, interestingly, as in the matter of the reportage on slavery in earliest medieval Japan, we acquire this knowledge perhaps most directly and pertinently from Chinese sources. Among the most trenchant of these observations comes to us from the writing-brush of Zhao Rugua 趙汝适 (1170–1231), whose critical importance lies in the fact that he is the author of the remarkable work *Zhufan zhi* 諸蕃志 (*Description of Foreign Peoples*; also known by the English-language titles *Records of Barbarous Nations* or *A Chinese Gazetteer of Foreign Lands*). Among the reports on numerous countries included therein is one describing the topography, products, and

---

[7] For more in brief on the adversarial history of relations between Vietnamese – that is, Đại Cồ Việt or Đại Việt – and Chams, see Kiernan, 2017 (repr. 2019): 142–44.

[8] On the lurid fetishism for southern women and girls of Yuè 越 maintained particularly by Chinese men of the Tang period, see Schafer, 1963: 44; Schafer, 1967: 56; Abramson, 2008: 21.

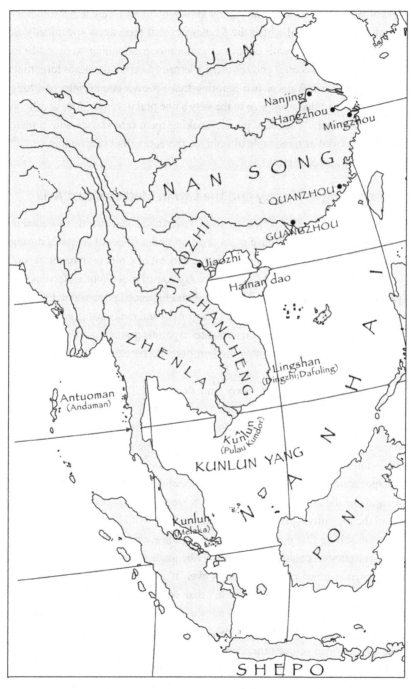

Figure 1 The Nanhai region, ca. 1225.

people of Annam 安南, as it was widely known by other foreigners throughout the medieval period, and which the Chinese of that time knew specifically as Zhanchengguo 占城國, with either designation corresponding territorially to what is now modern central and southern Vietnam. Seemingly either forgetting or selectively overlooking or just ignoring that his own countrymen had long engaged and continued to engage in the very same practice, the Chinese official Zhao observes that: "They buy people, making them into slaves, with a male youth being priced at three taels of gold, or the equivalent in aromatic wood" (Zhao, 1969: 1.3; see Figure 1).

Trafficking in Slavery and the Law in Medieval East Asia

The *Tang Code* (*Tang lü* 唐律), composed in 624 and subsequently modified in 627 and 637, so named because of its creation under imperial auspices during the Chinese Tang dynasty (618–907), is the earliest of Chinese dynastic sets of laws to be preserved intact.[9] As such, it greatly contributes to our understanding of premodern Chinese slavery in two vital and unprecedented ways. First, we should note that the *Tang Code* legally recognizes and ranks status groups, both aristocratic and servile. Second, it stipulates rigorous gradations of punishment based on one's status within either the family or the bureaucracy (Lewis, 2009: 50–52).

Thus, although considered lowly and demeaned from time immemorial, through the *Tang Code*, for the first time in history, the varieties of "base" (*jian* 賤) people became designated as such formally, in the laws. We learn, for example, that any crime that a "good" (*liang* 良) person – that is, free commoner – might commit against a "base" person was punished less severely than one perpetrated by someone base against someone non-base. As an indication of how rigid this dichotomization had become, we in fact also learn from the *Tang Code* of the illegality – punishable by strangulation – of kidnapping any "good" person and selling that person into slavery. Hence, under Tang law, at least in theory, free persons could only voluntarily be made to become slaves, which at least in normal times contributed to – even if it did not absolutely ensure – a division between "good" and "base" that was static (Lewis, 2009: 52–53; Hansen, 2015: 179–81).

Especially severe were those punishments meted out to either bondsmen or slaves who harmed or even threatened to harm their masters. The penalty for murdering one's master outright was death by decapitation. If the murder of the master was found to have occurred by accident, then means of execution – but not the penalty – was commuted to strangulation. For a slave to have been

---

[9] For the actual text in translation, in two volumes, see Johnson, 1979.

found even to have plotted to kill one's master, whether successfully or unsuccessfully, was punished with decapitation. Similarly, an uncovered plot to commit harm against any one of the relatives of one's master resulted in strangulation. By contrast, a master's killing of a slave for any offense without first securing government permission resulted merely in that master's beating. Any master who killed his slave with no provocation whatsoever was sentenced to one year of penal servitude (Benn, 2002: 40; Lewis, 2009: 53).

Furthermore, the imposed rigidity during the Tang dynasty of the divide between the "good" and the "base," the free and the unfree, classes made the idea of marriage between them untenable, if only asymmetrically so. Although there was little incentive to do so, nothing legally prevented free males from wedding unfree females. However, under no circumstances were male slaves to be allowed to marry the daughters of commoners. Those masters who permitted such unions to take place were subjected to two and a half years of penal servitude, and the marriages themselves were to be annulled (Benn, 2002: 40).

Therefore, we can see that the status of slaves in the *Tang Code*, even while at last recognized, was hardly a favorable one. Neither should we equate recognition with any advantage. As elsewhere in the medieval world, to the extent that laws were applicable to them, the slaves of Tang China were property. Indeed, the *Tang Code* afforded slaves a status identical to that of domestic animals and inanimate possessions. In accordance with past precedent of long standing, just as in the cases of horses, oxen, land, or houses, the purchase of a slave required a contract. However, given the fact that Tang authorities subjected virtually any activity related to economic development to a large measure of state control, such transactions were strictly regulated. Owing largely to the capacity to account for them as movable goods, in every case of the sale of either livestock or slaves, the government assessed a tax of 4 percent, with 3 percent being contributed by the buyer and 1 percent by the seller. This tax was then passed along for deposit in the imperial treasury (Pulleyblank, 1958: 212; Hansen, 1995: 40–42, 51–52, 90–91, 117).

Also codified within the formalized context of the *Tang Code* were the two types of slave that had customarily existed in China. These classifications consisted of official (*gong* 公; or, alternatively, state or public) slaves, being those owned by the government, and private (*si* 私) slaves, being those owned by individuals. Most official slaves were acquired through conquest, and this classification was largely comprised of either the once-free civilians or the captured soldiers of defeated enemy states or tribal peoples. Whereas they always represented a smaller proportion of the total in comparison to those cast into slavery as prisoners of war, populations of border-residing conquered aboriginal peoples and the dependents of criminalized or otherwise disgraced executed heads of families made up the bulk of the noncombatant civilians who became government slaves (Benn, 2002: 38–39). Private slaves, by contrast, were generally secured by a greater variety of means – legal as well as illegal – than were official slaves. Among the acceptable means of acquisition of private slaves was of course the sale and purchase of those already held by individuals. Commonplace especially in times of exigency was also the phenomenon of free but destitute individuals committing themselves to enslavement on the estates of the wealthy. Private slaves might furthermore be made of government slaves, resulting from their becoming gifts of the state to one or another favored private owner, such as a victorious general or comparably ranked military officer. However, among the illegal means was the brazenly outright kidnapping and enslavement of free citizens. Additionally, given the influence wielded by some that exceeded even that of the imperial lineage, powerful families would occasionally either steal or otherwise appropriate government slaves and convert them into private slaves of their own (Wang, 1953: 310–19).

Technically, these two types of slaves – one, official, and the other, private – differed little in either social status or legal position. We must nonetheless bear in mind that the drafters of the *Tang Code* had intended for its statutes to be principally applicable to an ethnically *Chinese* populace, within which were included slaves who were predominantly drawn from that overwhelmingly most populous segment of the population. Yet, beginning with the Tang, an irrepressible factor bearing on the legal position of slaves, whether official or private, was the whole matter of not only the circumstances *under* which but also the geographical points of origin *from* which they tended to be acquired.

Noteworthy over the course of the nearly three centuries of the Tang dynasty was a marked increase in foreigners acquired not only as customary official slaves but also as private slaves, and the region that supplied by far the greatest number of foreign private slaves was the one gradually emerging as the most prosperous – namely, the remote south of the empire. There, in the comparatively lawless terrain removed from the control of the central government, the approach of the slave traders was predatory and merciless. The favored tactic for procuring these various increasingly displaced aboriginal inhabitants of that same region was through kidnapping, precisely because the provisions of the *Tang Code* forbidding the enslavement of the free did not apply to them. Those merchants who traded in the frontier peoples of these distant southern prefectures considered them to be barbarous and irredeemably beyond the pale of Chinese civilization (Lewis, 2009: 169; Yang, 2022: 52). Therefore, we may surmise that their captors viewed these frontier populations as defenseless and entirely unprotected by any law that might have prohibited their abduction and sale, had there in fact been one.

Another of the many distinctions of the *Tang Code* is that it became privileged as serving as the template for all such subsequent codes of traditional law, not only in China in particular but throughout East Asia in general. In Korea, across the tenth through fourteenth centuries of duration of the Goryeo era, individuals of *nobi* status were legally permitted to marry only others of the same status, with the status of their offspring – inevitably, also *nobi* – determined along matrilineal lines. However, in time, given the social indistinguishableness between the *nobi* and the middle and/or commoner classes, with the exception of the ruling (*yangban* 양반; Chinese, *liangban* 兩班) class, which remained a caste apart, there were growing instances of cross-class intermarriage. In these circumstances, the law became interpreted *deterior condicio*, with the offspring of such unions between *nobi* and commoners invariably inheriting the status of the parent of lower rank, whether mother or father. Consequently, the main influence of the law on the *nobi* institution of slavery was in effect extra-legal, in that it profoundly reinforced its hereditary dimension, making it virtually inescapable by birth in a way that was not true in China (Patterson, 1982: 141–44; Kim, 2004: 153, 161).

However, we should note that, in contrast to Chinese tradition, laws in Korea could be employed to do more than merely preserve the slavery status quo. They were at least occasionally utilized even to subvert it. Perhaps the most illustrative example of the legal disruption of Korean slavery consists of the Slave Investigation Law or Act (*Nobi an'gŏmpŏp*; Chinese, *Nubi anjian fa* 奴婢按檢 法)[10] that was imposed in the mid-tenth century, specifically in 956, with the purpose of locating formerly free members of the population who had reportedly been subjected to enslavement in the course of the civil wars leading up to unification under the Goryeo dynasty (Salem, 1978: 91–92).

The Slave Investigation Law was imposed by the monarch Kwangjong 光宗 (r. 949–75), who has the distinction, in emulating the long-established Chinese convention, of being the first Korean king to assume the title of "emperor" (*hwangje* 皇帝).[11] We should note that neither magnanimity nor moral concern inspired the investigation. Instead, it was driven by the very practical and calculating desire on the part of the court to expand its revenue base by

---

[10] This law or act was promulgated nearly a half-millennium before the development of Hangul (*han'gŭl* or "Korean letters") in the mid-fifteenth century (precisely, the year 1443) of the Common Era. Consequently, at the time, Koreans themselves necessarily used Chinese characters to denote it.

[11] No other Korean king would again claim this title until 1879. See Henthorn, 1971 (repr. 1974): 89.

liberating erstwhile freehold-farming commoners from slavery and returning them to the tax registers. A corresponding impetus behind the measure was that of also maximizing the number of potential military recruits, who would otherwise be in private bondage and therefore exempt from service (Pratt, 2006: 87).

Kwangjong's initiative of what historian William Henthorn referred to as "transferring people from the nontaxable slave category to the taxable category of commoner" roused the anger of their elite slavers and naturally met with resistance, even leading to threats against the emperor himself. This opposition, despite coming as it did from many original supporters who had participated militarily in the founding of the dynasty, was ruthlessly crushed (Henthorn, 1971 [repr. 1974]: 89). Yet, the self-interested motivations behind it notwithstanding, beyond being a ploy to strengthen the hand of the state over that of the regional elite, we should also regard the Slave Investigation Law as part of a broader strategy effort pursued by the Goryeo regime to suppress the institution of at least private slavery in general, which it was reasonably successful in doing up until about the early twelfth century. Scholars resultantly concur that only upon the demise of the Goryeo dynasty in the late fourteenth century did the enslaved portion of the Korean total population exceed 10 percent (Seth, 2016: 86; Kye, 2021: 296–97).

We confront an entirely different situation with respect to slavery and its legal sanctions when we turn to medieval Japan. At the time that we may speak of the first categories of peoples identifiable as slaves there, Japan was without a formalized system of laws. Not before the end of the seventh and beginning of the eighth centuries did these mutually supportive sets of principles come into writing. Therefore, before then, among all of the classes, we cannot reasonably expect the status of slaves, the lowest of the low in any society, to have been specifically taken into account in documentary form. Nevertheless, like Korea, Japan also was much influenced by Chinese precedents and, in its specific case, such influence came in the form of the *ritsuryō* 律令 ("criminal and administrative" code; Chinese, *lüling*), which was a quasi-legal framework or system – rooted in Confucian–Daoist–Legalist ideological assumptions – that was focused most of all on the organization of the imperial court and its functions overtly along Chinese lines. Although it was more of an administrative reorganizational scheme than a set of actual legal statutes, the *Taihō* (Chinese, *Dabao* 大寶 or 大宝) *Code* of 701,[12] enacted in 702, as the best early expression to result from the *ritsuryō*, did lend at least some better definition to the standing of

---

[12] Albeit modeled on the Tang Chinese template, the *Taihō Code* was developed and instituted prior to the emergence and employment of the Japanese *kana* writing system in the ninth and tenth centuries of the Common Era.

slaves (Rodriguez, 1999: 101). However, the feature in Japanese law that it established that is perhaps most consistent of all with the Chinese model in its application to the citizenry broadly is the familiar distinction made between "good people" (*ryōmin* 良民) and "base people" (*senmin* or *semmin* 賤民). Furthermore, in Japan, each of these two basic caste divisions became further subdivided into four and five subcategories, respectively. To the extent that their existences were acknowledged by law at all, the last two subclassifications under the latter or "base" rubric were – again, familiarly, as was the situation both in China and Korea – official or public slaves, on the one hand, and private slaves, on the other (Sansom, 1931 [repr. 1962]: 220–21). Under this rubric of "base people," the last subgroup included, being effectively private chattel slaves, represented the largest category. They were owned principally by religious establishments, government officials, and sometimes well-off farmers and a slave of this type, "according to contemporary sources, had roughly the value of a strong horse or cow" (Toshiya, 1993: 426).[13]

In striking contrast to either China, or Korea, or Japan, when we seek to procure and convey even a modest assessment of the statuses of slavery and slaves in Vietnam during the medieval centuries, we are confronted with truly unbridgeable and insurmountable vacuities. The nature and the extent of the deficits are probably best articulated by the scholar Dang Trinh Ky, whose pioneering 1933 study still remains the best resource available to us on this specifically legal dimension of enslavement as an institution in medieval times. In it, Dang states, "Legislative collections of the dynasties before the Nguyen [Nguyễn; 1802–1945] have almost entirely disappeared" (Dang, 1933: 2). He further adds plaintively:

> There is nothing left of the *Book of Sorrows*, in particular, of the Ly dynasty, promulgated in 1042, nor of the collection of criminal laws of the Tran dynasty, promulgated in 1230. For a long time now, the famous Hông-Duc [Hồng Đức, from 1470 to 1497] Code, skillfully compiled during the reign of Lê-thanh-tôn [Lê Thánh Tông] (1483), has also been lost. Fortunately, there is one book left, recently discovered in the archives of Hue [Yuè], entitled *Code of the Lê dynasty* [1428–1786]. This work would have been published in about the year 1777. (Dang, 1933: 2)

Thus, in the case of Vietnam, we find that the available resources from which we can draw for insight into the state of slaving practices from a legal vantage point during medieval times are somewhat shy of even fragmentary.

---

[13] On the matter of ownership and utilization of private chattel slaves in medieval Japan, see also Sansom, 1931 (repr. 1962): 220–21.

However, given the fact that preserved subsequent legal statutes may well afford us knowledge of the tenor, flavor, and contents of lost earlier ones, all just might not be completely lost. For example, we can surmise that, in Vietnam, given the specificity with which it is delineated in the *Gia Long Code* (Vietnamese, *Bộ luật Gia Long*; Chinese, *Jialong fadian* 嘉隆法典) of 1812,[14] there is good reason to suspect that the distinction between true slavery and bond or debt service had already existed within the culture for a substantially long time. Even as a hypothetical, this circumstance may perhaps help in explaining why in Vietnam, just as in China, whereas the pawning and pledging of persons for a stipulated time was permitted, the outright sale of oneself or one's wife or relatives into slavery, which was always viewed as a permanent condition, was strictly prohibited (Dang, 1933: 18–20; Wilbur, 1943 [repr. 2016]: 85–90). Nevertheless, given the dearth of legal statutes we possess in the Vietnamese case, we should be cautious about extending this debt service versus slavery distinction too far back into earlier time, when it was doubtless subject to abuse. Moreover, there is evidence that suggests strongly that, over time, what was conceptualized as two distinct forms of bondage evolved to function in tandem in a kind of continuum.

Coercive Laboring Economies in Medieval East Asia

Entirely apart from how they had come to be procured, at least in China, the slaves of these two coexisting official and private designations within the premodern East Asian cultural sphere were perhaps distinguished most by the different work they were responsible for performing. As for the ethnically Chinese official slave in China, upon being "confiscated" or "seized" (*peimo* 配沒) or "registered" (*ji* 籍) and enslaved, the male dependents of an executed civilian patriarch were forced to perform arduous slave labor, typically for the remainder of what would be their much-shortened lives. As was also the case for a subset of their subjugated counterparts drawn from Indigenous peoples, those newly enslaved male descendants of the executed with the misfortune of being deemed by government authorities to be young enough were routinely castrated, so that they could then serve within the imperial palaces as eunuchs. Female members of these criminally besmirched families were also seized and subjected to the performance of slave labor, though – in contrast to the adult males – they

---

[14] Despite purportedly also incorporating substantive elements from the *Lê Code*, the *Gia Long Code* consisted of a largely wholesale adoption of China's Qing dynastic legal code, the *Great Qing Legal Code* (*Da Qing lülie* 大清律例) or simply the *Qing Code* (*Qing lü* 清律), which had been installed in the third year following the advent of the dynasty in 1647. See Dang, 1933: 8; Taylor, 2013: 401; Kiernan, 2017 (repr. 2019): 273. Although decreed in 1812, initial work on its composition began in 1811; its actual installation did not occur until 1815.

were forced to perform relatively light labor, such as rice-husking. These enslaved women could also be brought into the palaces as maids or, if regarded as being outstanding in attractiveness, they might actually be made imperial consorts. Moreover, as with any other slave, these female dependents could also be summarily given away by the emperor to his noble courtiers or, for the purpose of forging alliances, dispatched to other states (Wang, 1953: 301–10).

Private slaves in China were consigned to performing whatever tasks might be demanded of them by their masters. The possibilities included any and all tasks considered most grinding and deadly and, as in ages past, the toils of these slaves spanned the gamut from serf-like agricultural production to the disciplining – by means of beatings and torture – of fellow slaves. Owners could and did also subject their personal slaves with impunity to any punishment, even if it resulted in death and, whether maimed or as corpses, they could dispose of them at any time or in whatever way they wished (Wang, 1953: 310–19).

Such grim prospects notwithstanding, however, one prominent feature of private slavery in China, certainly by the fifteenth – and full terminal – century of the premodern era, is that it was becoming progressively domesticized, with many slave functions becoming redirected away from the tilling of land and toward providing household services (Wyatt, 2021: 281–84). This shift was in part a result of progressive urbanization. Yet, even on the still-proliferating rural manorial estates of the great landowning families of that time, private slaves labored in an assortment of domicile-connected roles, ranging from being personal attendants and groomsmen, to being gatekeepers and cooks, to being bodyguards and tomb surveillants, to being assistants in trade and farmhand entertainers. Indeed, over time, the large-scale creation of wealth became less of a rationale for private slave ownership than did ensuring basic comfort in daily life, together with the aspiration of promoting a prosperous image of the slave-owning family itself as representing people of means (Loewe, 1968 [repr. 2005]: 58–60; Wang, 1998: 179).

In Korea, just as in China, the distinction between official and private slavery was also observed. Nonetheless, we find that this bifurcation was far less crucial in Korea because there was little to no corresponding distinction in the types of coerced labor that slaves were forced to undertake. Whether during the Goryeo or the succeeding Joseon dynastic period, premodern Korean slavery almost exclusively identified with the enterprise of agrarian production, with farms themselves – initially, small rather than on the scale of plantations – owned either by individuals and public agencies in combination or by one or another branch of the government itself (Salem, 1978: 42–44).

However, aside from individuals and the state itself, another prime fixture of agricultural production and therefore, by necessity, controller of slaves in

Goryeo Korea via its commanding share of their ownership was the Buddhist church establishment (Lovins, 2022: 182–83). Indeed, from the standpoint of the Goryeo state, the incalculable surfeit in slave labor, in addition to landholdings, all of which was exempt from taxation, at the disposal of the numerous monasteries and temples constituting Buddhist ecclesiastical authority eventually came to pose a major problem. Among other factors, this amassed wealth in slaves as well as land led directly to anti-Buddhist sentiment and the sinking reputation and even the eventual persecution of the Buddhists in Korea (Seth, 2016: 98).

Moreover, such practices in Korea under the Goryeo dynasty as the escalating transfer of once-official slaves into Buddhist and therefore into private hands sharply contrasted with the situation in China in the same era, where monastery slaves already tended to be more of the private type (Salem, 1978: 44–48; Lewis, 2009: 217; Holcombe, 2011: 101). Similarly, it differed radically from prevailing circumstances of the time in Japan, where the private purchase of a slave of any type by a monk or nun or even the acceptance of one as a personal gift had long been strictly prohibited (Weinstein, 1999: 451). To combat some of these long-standing abuses by the Buddhists, the Goryeo government tended to focus on restricting the numbers of clerics, based on the logic that with fewer becoming monks or nuns, fewer slaves would come into the possession of the church. That said, at this time, the state prohibited slaves themselves and members of outcast groups from becoming monks or nuns (Seth, 2016: 98).

Nevertheless, in Korea, whether designated as official or private, whether government-owned or owned by an individual or the Buddhist church, slaves toiled predominantly as farm laborers, though some also served as domestic servants as well as artisans, and some moreover served possibly exclusively as painters. In these latter capacities, they likely contributed important technological innovations. Furthermore, despite the tribute owed and paid to their owners, some slaves also had independent incomes and enjoyed a fairly high degree of autonomy. This situation stemmed in part from the fact that, in contrast to China, under Korean law, slaves, even while categorized as "base people" (*cheonmin* or *ch'ŏnmin* 천민; Chinese, *jianmin*) were, at least by Joseon times of the fifteenth century, regarded as only a slightly more debased class of persons than the lowest order of "good people" (*yangmin* or *p'yŏngin* 양민; Chinese, *liangmin*).[15]

As Eugene Park observes, by early Joseon times, "an aristocratic landlord typically owned anywhere between 10 and 300 or more slaves," despite being

---

[15] See Salem, 1978: 4–6; Kim, 2004: 154–57; Seth, 2016: 62, 175, 180, 263, 307. *Yangmin* (*p'yŏngin*) is a more polite but less precise name for what by Joseon times was the class of *sangmin* 상민 ("commoners"; Chinese, *changmin* 常民).

a member of a class – the *yangban* – that constituted approximately 2 percent of the Korean population (Park, 2022: 148, 181). Whereas they were sometimes purchased, far more frequently slaves were either inherited or acquired as offspring of existing slaves, as the laws dictated that any child of a slave parent inherited the status of that parent, regardless of whether the status of the other parent was more elevated or even aristocratic. The work of slaves in the early Joseon period included caring for the household and weaving for those who owned them but, most importantly, tilling the land. Most of the enslaved lived separately from their masters, "as out-resident slaves who cultivated or managed their owners' land. From each out-resident slave, the owner annually collected a personal tribute of a bolt of cloth and paper money. During much of the fifteenth century, the state was mostly successful in prohibiting *yangban* landlords from taking over free cultivators' plots" (Park, 2022: 148).

Conforming to the patterns of slavery found elsewhere in the medieval world, those individuals enslaved in premodern Japan during such early eras as the Heian (794–1185) were principally war captives (Sansom, 1931 [repr. 1962]: 41). As of the early ninth century, these prisoners of war consisted overwhelmingly of rebellious groups of unassimilated tribal peoples of the "frontier" regions like the Emishi 蝦夷 or Ebitsu (also later called the Eko), who were inhabitants principally of the northeastern provinces of Dewa 出羽 and Mutsu 陸奥 (McCullough, 1999a: 30–32; Rizō, 1999: 646, 657–58, 660, 670). Without much initial success, the Japanese struggled against this outlying confederation of ethnic insurgents for thirty years, over the course of which there must have been much hostage-taking of at least its leaders. However, with military domination over them eventually achieved, vastly more prevalent as a Japanese tactic of Emishi subjugation than capture, not to mention enslavement, was their resettlement in dispersed restricted communities – not entirely unlike latter-day reservations – in which they could be controlled (McCullough, 1999a: 30–32; Rizō, 1999: 670–71; Farris, 2009b: 82–83).

In contrast to the gradual continuous expansion in numbers on par with their counterparts in China and especially in Korea within this same early medieval period,[16] the population of endogenous Japanese slaves fluctuated greatly as a function of the disruptions of natural calamities such as earthquakes, flooding, drought, pestilence, and associated famine but, even more importantly, the inflictions of endemic armed conflict, conducted largely on the part of contending *daimyo* (Japanese, *daimyō* 大名; literally, "great name[s]") elites, the feudal landowning magnate-warlords of premodern Japan. The more chaos

---

[16] The scholarly consensus is that this increase in slaves over the course of the medieval period was in terms of real numbers only for China but in terms of real numbers as well as percentage of the overall population for Korea.

attributable to these factors but chiefly to the latter, the more slaves were produced (Farris, 2009b: 182, 188). Provincially, farmers and artisans among the slave class were either bound in a serf-like manner to the land or restricted to hereditary occupations (Kiley, 1999: 238). Nevertheless, these constraints notwithstanding, the latter group of craftspeople limited to hereditary trades – the *shinabe* 品部 (artisan groups) – gradually rose to occupy positions in status independent of landed authority (Toshiya, 1993: 426; McCullough, 1999b: 166–67).

For our best knowledge of the prevailing conditions of slavery in medieval Vietnam, which was by this time called the kingdom of Đại Việt (modern-day northern Vietnam), we turn by necessity to the first – that is, the thirteenth – of the two centuries of the Trần dynasty.[17] With the acquisition of slaves by that time having become primarily the prerogative of the state, the early Trần rulers acquired slaves in various ways, including self- or voluntary enslavement, and in large numbers. Moreover, given the proximity of Đại Việt to China and the easing in hostile relations between the two states at that time, enslaved men and women by the reputed "hundreds of thousands" were kidnapped and trafficked across their commonly shared border (Kiernan, 2017 [repr. 2019]: 165).

However, for the Trần leadership, the real utility of having massive numbers of slaves available showed itself during the Mongol Wars, when Đại Việt succeeded in repelling three successive attempted invasions of the enemy, in 1258, 1285, and from 1287 into 1288.[18] Amidst the exigencies of these existential incursions, the regime sometimes mobilized entire armies composed of slaves. Yet, perhaps most important for our purposes, as K. W. Taylor observes, "In the thirteenth century, slavery was not a particularly bad fate. Slaves were generally well cared for and, in wartime, served their masters loyally. The condition of slaves, and also that of peasants, would change dramatically in the fourteenth century when, lacking the kind of leadership provided by the first three kings, [the Trần] government faltered" (Taylor, 2013: 122).

Slave Social Organization, Culture, and Identity in Medieval East Asia

In China, from the time of the Song dynasty (960–1279) onward, the terminology for the "good" (*liang*) people actually referred to most ordinary Chinese – known as the common folk (*min* 民) since ancient times – of all occupations. As historian Frederick W. Mote judiciously observed, by Song times, those legally

---

[17] For more on the transition from the Lý dynasty to the Trần dynasty, see Kiernan, 2017 (repr. 2019): 166–67.

[18] Champa suffered a separate invasion, also unsuccessful for the Mongols, between 1282 and 1284. See Taylor, 2013: 133; Kiernan, 2017 (repr. 2019): 169.

designated as "base" (*jian*) people had come to be included under this rubric primarily through their engagement in "debased" occupations, such as prostitutes, barbers, and – through religious influences such as Buddhism and its expressed prohibition on the taking of animal life – butchers. Mote, moreover, judiciously estimated the average representative percentage of the total population at any given point in time of this base subdivision to have been an inconsequential 3 to 5 percent (Mote, 1999: 366).

On the one hand, to be sure, there were many contexts in which the "base people" and their offspring were discriminated against, with their technical ineligibility for the long-established but newly perfected civil service examinations of the state being merely one of them. However, on the other hand, as Mote also contended, especially with the rise of the unique Song situation, now for the first time in China's long history bereft of a hereditary aristocracy and hence more egalitarian as a society overall, other less stigmatizing contexts did in fact remain accessible to them. These were newly arisen contexts, often commercial, in which they might frequently endeavor to and oftentimes succeed, at least economically, in evading such discrimination. As a result, it is suggested that baseness became at least as much or more occupationally determined during the Song than it was, as in the manner of the past, delineated by class (Mote, 1999: 366–67). Yet we must simultaneously bear in mind that the classic Chinese hierarchical four-tiered class system of scholar-officials (*shi* 士), peasants (*nong* 農), artisans (*gong* 工), and merchants (*shang* 商) itself, which had been operative since the latter part of the Zhou dynasty (1045–221 BCE) and never inclusive of slaves, was in essence occupationally derived.

Nonetheless, without question, the social tendency most critical in influencing slavery as a practice in premodern China was an incremental process of attenuation of the figurative distance separating the customary classes that led perhaps inevitably to its domestication. Such was the case from the beginning of the Song on through to the end of the imperial era, and this process likely ensued for many reasons – but especially salient is the fact that so very much of what we do now know about slaving conventions during the Song comes from extant primary source documentation that focuses principally on the labor functions of slaves. These documents strongly suggest that most slaves of this transitional period functioned neither as penal nor agricultural workers but instead domestically. They therefore formed the lowest stratum of a broadly defined subclass of household servants, and thus lived and died in circumstances of closer intimacy with their masters than at any prior time in history.

In Korea, where they had since later Goryeo times come to serve as the collective backbone of the overall economy, slaves formed the bottom-most substratum of a three-class hierarchical social structure. However, it was a framework in which they were definitely included and one in which – because of their essentialness – they became beneficiaries in ways that was never the case for their counterparts in China. Whether public or private in designation, very nearly all of the Korean *nobi* were owned by the *yangban* ruling elite, which, as a distinct class, never exceeded constituting any more than about one-tenth of the population throughout the premodern period. In the effort to establish a psychic connection between the hereditary nature of *nobi* status and upward loyalty to themselves, the *yangban* developed and subjected their slaves as a class to elaborate arguments of moral suasion, all of which were intended to reinforce social immobility in what was already a socially immobile system. Arguably, much success was achieved by these rationalizations because, in combination with other factors, in the course of the passage from Goryeo to Joseon completed by the early fifteenth century, this discourse seems to have helped facilitate a sizeable numerical increase in slaves from about 10 to as much as 30 percent of the Korean population (Palais, 1996: 15, 35, 41, 55, 60, 68, 208–10, 217–25, 238; Palais, 1998: 34–38; Kim, 2004: 160; Holcombe, 2011: 146; Lovins, 2022: 196, 198–99).

According to Eugene Park, best estimates suggest that by the sixteenth century, the overall population of Korea was more than 10 million persons and by the end of the seventeenth century, was between 10 and 12 million (Park, 2022: 180–81). Yet there are some strong indications that slaves were not before those times very evenly distributed throughout the country because if slave labor was insufficient during the early Joseon, then *yangban* would simply commandeer local tenant farmers, taking half the harvest of each. The roles of slaves in the management of these aristocratic estates could also vary in early Joseon times. "Some yangban managed their land personally by maintaining residences and storage near their holdings. Still, for the most part, they relied on local relatives and, from time to time, dispatched their personal slaves to provide supervision" (Park, 2022: 148). However, by the late fifteenth century, with the proliferation of aristocratic landholders and the corresponding increase in dispossessed, impoverished commoners, the latter were subsumed and treated effectively as agrarian slaves of the former (Park, 2022: 148).

As for Japan, aside from their most subordinate of ranked positions in the aforementioned *ritsuryō* system, once again, we know little of social dynamics in which slaves might have been involved in premodern times. Some substantial scholarly attention, however, has been directed toward the third-ranking classification under the "base people" or *senmin* rubric because such persons are known to have been owned people, who, at least originally, occupied an indeterminate position between "the unfree and the half-free," being called "house persons" (*kenin* 家人 or, also, *yatsuko* in Japanese; Chinese, *jiaren*)

(Asakawa, 1903 [repr. 1963]: 82–86).[19] Originally, such "house persons" were privately owned servants, who were better off than the official and private slaves ranked below them because whereas they could be inherited, they could not be sold. They also evidently could participate in the social life of the families by which they were owned as well as have families of their own.

On the one hand, just as it was the foundational premise in Korea and Japan, the fundamental Chinese paradigm of a society divided into "good" and "base" people was, to be sure, by medieval times if not already for centuries earlier, operationally accepted in Vietnam (Dang, 1933: 24). On the other hand, it is also starkly evident, at least in relative terms, that the Vietnamese came, over time, to view this division as vastly more permeable and even porous than did their East Asian counterparts. Still, the primary-source documentation on which we can rely in the Vietnamese case remains comparatively scarce, forcing us to seek understanding of the social rudiments of the earlier slaving practices mostly through the lens of subsequent history. Even so, in advancing our knowledge of slavery in Vietnam as best we can, we very possibly profit most from turning first to yet another dynastic transition: that occurring in the change from the Trần to the Lê.

The Lê dynasty is also known in history as the Later Lê dynasty and, in spanning from 1428 to 1789, it was the longest-lived of those to rule over Vietnam. From its very founding, in every sense, the Lê represented an attempted reset in terms of its vision of the Việt polity. The reimagining posed was not only in contradistinction to that of the preceding native Trần regime but also in reaction to the intervening one posed by the overlordship of the Chinese Ming dynasty (1368–1644), which had occupied the country from 1407 up until 1428.[20]

The Lê regime was eager to recruit even those individuals into its ranks who – essentially, as defectors – had elected to serve the Chinese Ming dynasty and, in order to do so, slavery became a source of leverage in bringing those former traitorous members of the elite back into the fold. Upon transferring their loyalty to the Lê as legitimate successors of the Trần, conditionally, even those guilty of complicity with the Ming occupiers were allowed to redeem their reacquired but captive slaves, along with their wives and children, via ransoming (Taylor, 2013: 187). However, probably foremost among the cardinal aims of the reforms of dynastic founder Lê Lợi (Chinese, Li Li 黎利)

---

[19] See also Hall, 1966: 34–35, 251. Hall called these persons "slaves" but, given that the term evolved over succeeding centuries to mean "housemen," in the sense of "retainers," the problem with so firm a designation as this is exposed within his own study.

[20] On the Ming occupation, see Taylor, 2013: 173–77; Kiernan, 2017 (repr. 2019): 194–97. On the lingering border-related tensions following the Ming withdrawal, see Shin, 2007: 91–104.

(ca. 1384/85–1433) that were instituted was that of putting abandoned and confiscated land back into production. In the process, slavery became one of the cultural institutions subjected to a kind of muddling, such that it became, under the Lê, in many ways, indistinguishable from serfdom. Or, as K. W. Taylor puts the matter, "There came an end to large estates farmed by slaves or peasants in a serf-like status. Instead, villages were organized on the basis of free peasants with enough land to support their families and pay taxes." (Taylor, 2013: 187).

Clearly, under these changed socioeconomic conditions, whereas there was no institutional abandonment of slavery, without question, many of its most pernicious effects in Vietnam must have been greatly mitigated. For example, much in the mold of the then-ancient *Tang Code* of China, as the scholar John Whitmore observes, "the Lê Code forbade the powerful, whether private or public, to take freemen into their service (articles 165–68, 171). The kidnapping of freemen was also explicitly forbidden (articles 365, 453, 536)" (Whitmore, 1984: 302).[21] However, probably the clearest indicator of improved circumstances for slaves was their enhanced standing before the law in relation to their masters. We know, for example, that according to the *Lê Code*, the murdering of a slave by the master required justification because, upon investigation, "[i]f the slave had committed no fault, the master murderer would be sentenced to servitude" (Dang, 1933: 23; Patterson, 1982: 191–92).

Gender, Enslavement, and Trafficking in Medieval East Asia

Our knowledge of the conduction of slavery in China during the Song dynasty and thereafter also departs from what we have heretofore come to expect because of the progressive association of enslaved status more with women than with men. Although it is reflexively associated with periods of comparative stability accompanied by prolonged peace, we must also acknowledge that this emergent trend oftentimes unfolded against the backdrop of warfare. Therefore, it is certainly tenable that it was a tendency abetted and even accelerated by the violence associated with war. Indeed, its continuance with hardly a ripple of disruption during the shockingly near-instantaneous change to the Southern Song dynasty (1127–1279) and the excruciatingly protracted seven decades of assault on China and surrounding territories by the Mongols, from 1215 until 1288, fully attests to this truth.

As important as it is undeniable, however, is that a gendered transformation in the normative Chinese mental image of the typical slave – one that departed from that of the male prisoner of war of Tang times and earlier to reconstitute itself as that of the female housebound slave of initially early Song but also subsequent times – did occur. Upon reflection, this transmogrification is perhaps

---

[21] On the *Tang Code* as the earliest and most venerated template for the *Lê Code*, see Tran, 2018: 7.

unsurprising because it is so familiar to us, for perhaps no image of enslavement in premodern China more readily and frequently springs forth in the modern Western mind than that of the concubine (*qie* 妾). Always exploited exclusively by a ruling and/or economic elite, in the Song, just as in every other Chinese epoch, whether earlier or later, her cardinal labor function has been always the same – namely, consisting of the imperative of the production of a male heir for the perpetuation of the patriarchal family line.

Yet, her sexual servitude notwithstanding, though she could conceivably be thought of as such, we are cautioned to realize that, unlike us, Chinese of medieval times neither regularly nor habitually conceptualized the concubine as a slave (Ebrey, 2002 [repr. 2003]: 39–40). Indeed, Song law, drawing for guidance on the earlier statutes of the *Tang Code*, stipulated that men may only take women of "respectable" (*liang*) status as concubines. Slaves and bond-maids were by definition of "base" (*jian*) status and thereby deemed to be not of a suitable class. Thus, we find that concubines were expected to be of good standing before the law because they – in contrast to slaves or bondmaids – were regarded as loosely "married" to their masters (Bossler, 2012: 58–60).

Nevertheless, if only tacitly, Song law simultaneously acknowledged the right of sexual access of the master to the servile women in his household as well as the importance of producing descendants to uphold the Chinese family system. Consequently, interlaced among the laws were numerous qualifications, such as a provision that, for example, permitted a bondmaid who was manumitted by her master in advance of giving birth to a child to be elevated to the status of a concubine. In this way and others that circumvented the strictness of the laws, a particularly "favored" bondmaid and occasionally even a slave might succeed in being raised by their masters to the respectable status of a concubine.

Despite the progressive preeminence of the concubine in our notions of premodern Chinese slavery, in connection with gender, we would be remiss not to account also, at least briefly, for the enduring presence of the eunuch (*huanren* 宦人). These being individuals who had either been forced or who had elected voluntarily to undergo the irreversible neutering procedure of castration, we are probably most readily inclined to categorize eunuchs as official male slaves, albeit of a very specialized type.[22] However, as in the case of the concubine, given that their view was more instrumentalist than our own modern

---

[22] For more expressly on that life-altering procedure, see Mitamura, 1992: 28–35. Premodern Korea and Vietnam also maintained the institutions, with both modeled on that of China, wherein eunuchs were utilized by occupants of the throne and their relatives. For details on the process in Korea, see Kim, 2009: 116–27. A unique feature of the Vietnamese practice, especially during the Lý and Trần dynastic eras, is that nearly all eunuchs were self-produced, products of their own castrations. See Taylor, 2013: 121–22.

one, with a mind mainly toward how individuals socially or institutionally functioned, Chinese observers of premodern times were not likely to have regarded eunuchs as properly slaves at all. Given their inability to reproduce, the prime original function of eunuchs was that of trusted servants within and vigilant sentries without the imperial harems, thus ensuring that the progeny of the emperors was in fact theirs (Dawson, 1972: 84). Thus, we should neither be surprised that their history in China is a very long one – spanning at least three millennia – nor that the chief venue of their activity has been almost exclusively that of the imperial household quarters (Holcombe, 2011: 106). Thus, while being de facto slaves because they lacked self-determination in any sense, eunuchs – owing to their proximity to rulers via lives lived in the palace compound – were regarded as occupying a privileged space apart, by being high-placed, if often corrupt, nefarious, and manipulative servants of the emperor (Wyatt, 2021: 290–92; see Figure 2).

Figure 2 Anonymous. Group of eunuchs. Mural from the tomb of Prince Zhanghuai, 706, Qianling Mausoleum, Shaanxi.

Gender also much influenced the developmental course of and especially the trafficking in slavery in Korea. Moreover, it was a factor that clearly led to an exploitive focus particularly on the *bi* side – that is, the female slaves – within the *nobi* system. We know that throughout the Goryeo period, enslaved women, because of their reproductive potential, were actually more prized than their male counterparts, commanding higher prices than did enslaved men. As the numbers of mixed *nobi*–non-*nobi* marriages increased over the course of the dynasty, this differential in value doubtless heightened, given that most such unions involved *yangmin* or commoner husbands and *nobi* or slave wives. However, even in those uncommon cases in which the genders in the union might be reversed, because of the dictate of the inheritance of lower status, all children produced were necessarily *nobi* (Kim, 2004: 159, 161–62). Needless to say, with the transition to the Joseon dynasty, this augmentation of those bearing slave status by natural means would have profound consequences for the *nobi* component as a portion of the Korean population overall, leading – by the mid-fourteenth century – to its full conversion from what had been a slave-owning society to a slave society (Salem, 1978: 151).

In Japan of premodern times, as best we can discern, the connection between gender and slavery was most pronounced in the realm of what we would today call sex trafficking. Prominent among the social groups that populated mid-to-late Heian times were cohorts of skilled itinerant women entertainers, whose professional services extended to sexual liaisons with elite male patrons. Most conspicuous among these groups were the *asobi* 遊女 (also pronounced *yūjo*) or *yūkun* 遊君, meaning literally "roaming women" or "wandering princesses," who were most frequently to be found entertaining travelers at seaports and river portages (Goodwin, 2007: 1–5). These women are said to have received their traditions in entertainment by indirect appropriation from China, perhaps by means of immigrants via Korea, with these being places where – in either case – such performers were definitely of "base" status and therefore potentially slave backgrounds.[23] Moreover, a major open question stemming from linguistic imprecision remains that of whether the *asobi* were regarded as principally entertainers or prostitutes in their time (Goodwin, 2007: 2–4).

---

[23] In Korea, already by Goryeo times, the profession of the *kisaeng* or *ginyeo* (Korean, 기녀; Chinese, *jinü* 妓女) had emerged. Being "singing and dancing girls," these women, despite being accomplished in the more refined entertainment arts of the courtesan, were drawn almost exclusively from slave or outcast families. They are considered by some to be the forerunners or at least influencers of the Japanese geisha of early modern and later times. For more on the *kisaeng* by early Joseon times, see Park, 2022: 154.

Furthermore, even if it were answerable, the challenge of conclusively interpreting what *asobi* status must have been would still extend beyond that of resolving the lingering question of primary function. On the one hand, in Japan, even if technically classified as social undesirables, many of these *asobi* – exploiting the fluid sexual mores as well as the relative autonomy afforded to women by the eleventh century of the Heian era – had nonetheless possessed modest but respectable social status before entering the trade (Goodwin, 2007: 8–10, 11–15, 132–33). Yet, on the other hand, in part because of its lingering intersection with the subversive and thus often suspiciously regarded tradition of the shamans, who were invariably members of the underclass, the status of the *asobi* calling itself declined markedly over time (Goodwin, 2007: 12, 13, 84, 87–91, 93, 96–103, 113–14, 118–19). Consequently, from even about as early as the end of the tenth century onward, the *asobi* profession was increasingly seen as interfaced, if not inextricably intertwined, with the slave trade, if only because the latter provided a lucrative market from which young girls could be continually purchased for and channeled into the former (Ruch, 1990 [repr. 1997]: 525). Additionally, as the groundbreaking scholarly inquiry into historical conventions of Japanese slavery of Maki Hidemasa makes clear, inasmuch as their services were always purchasable for a price, the *asobi* were, in their time, regarded as saleable human beings (Maki, 1971: 189–200).

With respect to the influence of gender on slaving practices in Vietnam, we should expect at least some differences from the cases of medieval China, Korea, and Japan, if only because Đại Cồ Việt and subsequently Đại Việt, in a manner conforming to Southeast Asian precedent generally, each fostered cultures that were customarily much closer than those of the others of the East Asian region of the world, in medieval times as well as very likely before and certainly since then, to being ones of gender parity (Taylor, 1983: 130; Murphey, 1996 [repr. 1997]: 173). Proto-Vietnamese of the earlier Lạc Việt culture had firmly maintained a levirate system, wherein surviving brothers typically married the childless widows of their deceased brothers, until the third century of the Common Era and it persisted incidentally for centuries longer (Taylor, 1983: 130; Taylor, 2013: 20; Kiernan, 2017 [repr. 2019]: 51–52, 91, 206). Moreover, despite the early impress of the patriarchal cultural norms imposed on them prior to the first of their several liberations from Chinese overlordship in 935, the people who emerged as the Vietnamese had long practiced gender-based conventions that were, in many ways, antithetical to the institution of patriarchy. We may note that, among other examples, since indeterminably ancient times, Việt women had possessed rights of property inheritance; accepted marriage practice had been and continued to be matrilocal, with a bride-price paid by the groom and/or his family rather than a dowry received; and offspring – whether male or female – were permitted to inherit through their mothers (Murphey, 1996 [repr. 1997]: 173; Taylor, 2013: 20, 301; Kiernan, 2017 [repr. 2019]: 75, 206). Indeed, only with the promulgation of the *Lê Code* in the early fifteenth century, modeled to such a great extent as it was on that of Ming China, did these age-old Việt prerogatives conferred to women become seriously confronted or compromised. Moreover, we must see other aspects of the *Lê Code*, which incorporated still earlier Tang conventions, as posing only the most extreme of challenges and therefore setbacks to the customary autonomy that Vietnamese women had enjoyed (Kiernan, 2017 [repr. 2019]: 206).

We of course might anticipate that the ramifications emanating from such a continuous and entrenched tradition of Việt female autonomy should very likely be as consequential as they were exceptional. One of the most salient of these ramifications is that, whereas she most assuredly did exist throughout Vietnamese history, nonetheless, the concubine as a cultural fixture was both less prevalent and less uniformly dispersed throughout the classes than was the case in China, being instead confined largely though not exclusively to royal and ruling elite circles (Taylor, 2013: 67, 69, 91, 94, 111, 123, 224, 372; Kiernan, 2017 [repr. 2019]: 229, 268, 273, 541; Tran, 2018: 72, 96–98, 104). That said, however, despite being less commonplace and less widely represented throughout even the uppermost strata of the society, we can little question that the concubine of medieval Vietnam was oftentimes a woman of pedigreed status who, through no fault of her own, had become consigned to enslaved status. As Dang Trinh Ky retrospectively remarked, "The truly regular source of slavery in ancient Annam was judicial condemnation" (Dang, 1933: 10), and he also added regarding the frequently highborn women it befell that, "[t]hey were originally daughters of the guilty, condemned as slaves, ... and distributed by the state to the mandarins as concubines" (Dang, 1933: 41).[24] Yet, interestingly, there seems, on balance, also to have been an abiding cultural recognition of the factors deleterious to autonomy that so regularly and inescapably precipitated the fall into concubinage. Such recognition perhaps partly explains why Vietnam, in subsequent times, developed the East Asian region's sole embedded tradition of concubine manumission – with it becoming a convention wherein, upon the birth of a child by the master, a concubine was automatically granted free status (Patterson, 1982: 230).

---

[24] See also Tran, 2018: 111–14.

Family, Age, and Bondage in Medieval East Asia

Scant evidence, if any, attests to Chinese slaving and human trafficking traditions generally endeavoring to preserve those held in bondage as familial units. As was largely the case elsewhere, an operative expectation of enslavement was the severance of kinship bonds and such was indeed the overall practice in China aside from one overt exception, with it being one that was limited exclusively to the very early medieval period of the Northern Wei dynasty (386–534). During that time, the rulers, who were themselves foreign Xianbei 鮮卑 Tuoba 拓跋 tribesmen rather than ethnic Chinese,[25] might be inclined to gift a special category of official slave as a reward to favored private owners, with those typically being victorious generals or comparably ranked military officers. Interestingly, what distinguished these slaves, who thereupon were delivered from government into private servitude, is that they consisted of entire "slave households" (*lihu* 隸戶) (Wang, 1953: 318). However, aside from this one rather exceptional example to the contrary, one that is arguably well outside the dominant tilt of the system overall, Chinese models of enslavement have been overwhelmingly predicated on the destruction of the bonds of kinship of those enslaved.

The Chinese also seem to have been traditionally disposed to favor the early imposition of slavery, such that, throughout premodern times, the phenomenon of childhood slavery was commonplace to the point of being ubiquitous. Inevitably, these were circumstances in which the natal unit was destroyed. While it favored the interests of productivity, this subjection of the youthful to slavery was frequently precipitated by forces of disruption instead of profit, wherein the parents of families driven to destitution by natural or manmade disaster would sell their children into slavery, for the sake of the survival of the latter. Yet child enslavement in China could also be motivated not by duress but simply out of the desire for families to advance their own fortunes at the *expense* of their offspring. In this connection, inasmuch as we are persuaded to accept it as a true condition of slavery, eunuchism is quite illustrative. In instances too numerous ever to know, given the enhanced chances for survival when the procedure was performed in youth, it was in fact the parents who chose to commit their sons, while they were still in their infancy, to this path into servitude (Kim, 2009: 168).

---

[25] The Xianbei were an ancient nomadic proto-Mongolic people, once residing in the eastern Eurasian steppes of present-day Mongolia, Inner Mongolia, and northeastern China. The tribes rose to ascendancy in China when, under the leadership of their Tuoba (also Tabgach or Tabgatch) imperial clan, they established the Northern Wei dynasty (386–534 CE).

Without question, the slaves of the medieval *nobi* system of Korea, in contrast to their counterpart *nubi* in China, possibly because of the rigidly caste-like quality of slave status that eventually emerged, even amidst bondage, enjoyed considerably more familial cohesion and integrity. We know that those members of the agrarian *nobi* not responsible for directly cultivating the domain of their masters – that is, the large tribute-paying subclass – bore a close semblance to Korean commoners, in that they "were permitted their own houses, families, land, and fortunes, and were registered officially as independent family units" (Kim, 2004: 155). The fact that the overwhelming preponderance of slaves in Korea had been born as slaves must also have had a nullifying effect on age as a variable within the slaving context. The invariantly inherited nature of slave status doubtless rendered all issues of one's relative age – and therefore one's accrued time spent within it, which was nearly always from birth – moot (See Figure 3).

Of the very little we know in socio-familial terms about the slaves of premodern Japan in general and the class of *senmin* – of which they composed the lowest two tiers – in particular, even whether they were consistently allowed to establish families is questionable. Extant household registers as well as other records of as early as the eighth century hardly mention the *senmin*, let alone those of their cohort classified at the two lowest levels as slaves, official and private (*kunuhi* 公奴婢 and *shinuhi* 私奴婢; Chinese, *gong nubi* and *si nubi*), and legal statutes of then and subsequent centuries are similarly uninformative. From this paucity of comment, we can infer that, from that early time onward, their numbers were just never large enough to be consequential, with best estimates for the agricultural *senmin* as a subgroup of the overall population placed at no more than 10 percent and probably less than even 5 percent (Sansom, 1958: 111; Sansom, 1931 [repr. 1962]: 41, 171). If true, then we can deduce that they could never have been responsible for any meaningfully substantive portion of Japanese agrarian production and we must therefore conclude that the likelihood that they were afforded such a bare amenity as only a life of subsistence for sustaining themselves as a viable family unit seems quite suspect. Or, to state the matter another way, even though he is more charitable than past estimators about the fraction of the overall population they might have constituted, as historian of medieval Japan William Wayne Farris informs us, "eighth- and ninth-century Japanese society was comprised of about 5–10 percent slaves (*nuhi*), whose families could be broken up by sale, a condition probably lowering fertility for a significant portion of the populace" (Farris, 2009a: 86).

As was mentioned earlier in relation to slavery in medieval Vietnam, despite the culturally recognized distinction that was customarily drawn, especially in

Figure 3 *Genre Scenes* (detail), by Cheong Sichang (Cheng Shichang), active
1480s. National Museum of Korea, Seoul.

legal terms, between the two forms of bondage, much of the relatively meager evidence that does survive suggests, on the contrary, that debt service and actual enslavement came over time not only into a coexistent but also interfaced relationship. Unfortunately, we can only surmise what must have been the influence of this interfacing on the social contours of medieval Vietnamese slavery indirectly and obliquely, and we must do so by extrapolation via the only extant opus that sheds light on these matters in the form of the *Gia Long Code*. In many respects, we will discover that the closest analogue to the Vietnamese situation is probably that which unfolded in Korea, particularly during the transition from the Goryeo to the Joseon dynasty at the end of the fourteenth and beginning of the fifteenth centuries.

The crucial point of comparability between what we know of medieval Korea and what we can only reasonably theorize about Vietnam in medieval times is that there genuinely does appear to have been some potential for familial life among slaves in some form. However, to reiterate, we know neither precisely how far back in time it extends nor, for that matter, exactly what form it took. Still, assuredly, from a logical standpoint in terms of addressing what this prospective familial life of the medieval Viêt enslaved must have been like, we may turn to the *Gia Long Code*. We thereupon find that, by its admittedly later times, if not extending back so far as to those of the fifteenth through eighteenth centuries of the Lê dynastic period, marriage between slaves was considered lawful, with its registration being retained by the master as head of the family and a copy deposited with the district magistrate. We are further informed by Dang Trinh Ky that the Roman *contubernium*, being the sanctioned quasi-marital relationship between a free citizen and a slave or between two slaves, "without rights or guarantees, had no equivalent in Annam." Yet, even if a slave were to enter into such a relationship, the master, who was ostensibly empowered to terminate it if he objected, could in principle inflict no punishment. Pronouncing the appropriate sentence for the transgression was entirely the prerogative of the magistrate (Dang, 1933: 23).

Enslavement by Outsiders in Medieval East Asia: The Jingkang Incident and Aftermath

With the arguable exception of Japan, depending on how one wishes to characterize its occupation under United States military forces from 1945 to 1952, each of the constituent countries of what we today regard as East Asia, for a substantive period, has suffered the domination of some greater or lesser portion of its territory – and, consequently, its populace – by an ethnoracial outsider people. However, over the course of its post-unification history of nearly two millennia, only China has suffered this ignominious fate during its medieval centuries on multiple occasions in succession. Thus, on account of this unique premodern developmental experience, in which slavery inescapably plays some role, as well as its position as the cultural preeminence and its conventions of documentation, unsurprisingly, China is the best positioned among the entities composing East Asia to illustrate the vicissitudes undergone, the injuries inflicted, and the indignities endured when one medieval culture fell prey to enslavement by another.

What follows is a deliberation on this infused interconnection between war and slavery as it most notoriously transpired as a phenomenon during the latter stage of the Chinese midimperial era – that is, by Western calibration, during the twelfth through fourteenth centuries. However, the uniqueness of the events recounted lies not just in the fact of its circumscription to these waning centuries of the extensive period in question. The story here told presents us also with a uniquely fascinating and revealing inversion. Such is the case because we find that, in every instance considered, the Chinese were never the perpetrators but instead the victims.

This reversal of normal circumstances in which the Chinese were not enslavers of surrounding non-Chinese peoples but enslaved by them is rife with implications, and this situation thereby provides us with an uncommonly informative lens for scrutinizing the synergistic affine relationship between war and slavery. Through it, the legacy forged by the untold incidences of this particular dynamic in violence becomes exposed through the historical episodes attesting to its prevalence. As a result, we come to see and appreciate just how momentously consequential the paradigm of defeat in war as a prelude to enslavement has been in the construction of subsequent Chinese notions of identity. Moreover, emerging as equally apparent is how fully these wanton acts of past enslavement, to which those most militarily weakened and vulnerable were subjected, have exerted residual sociopolitical influence on the collective memory, lasting well into contemporary times. Quite understandably but nonetheless tragically, this legacy, in all of its bitterness, has also profoundly impinged on the shaping of the frequently contemptuous modern Chinese outlook reserved for and demonstrated toward formerly hostile neighboring peoples, with many of these groups having long since come to constitute distinctly recognizable ethnic minorities within the boundaries of present-day China proper itself.

Unfreedom – like all other conditions of human challenge and deprivation – has a tremendously long history in China. However, with that story incapable of being told or even known in full, let us resort to a consideration of those examples that we can regard as most prominently illustrative of that history in its midimperial expression. Given the intimate association of unfreedom with war contended above, that we should commence our analysis with a pivotal episode of violence arising in that venue is perhaps to be expected. Thus, having reasonable confidence that we can nearly always best begin to understand and appreciate medieval unfreedom at its most extreme by considering it as it unfolded against the backdrop of armed conflict, we commence our analysis here with the series of harrowingly gruesome altercations that have come very specifically to be remembered as the early twelfth-century Jin–Song wars. These struggles were waged between the overmatched initial Song (960–1127) dynasty of the predominantly ethnic Han 漢 Chinese (the same group that demographically dominates China today) and its besieging tribal Jurchen (in Chinese, Nüzhen 女眞) counterpart, in the form of the newly emergent Jin (1115–1234) dynasty (Tao, 1977: 3–24).[26] In endeavoring to reconstruct this context of mortal strife, we can hardly select a better event to illustrate the bitter realities of subjugation and bondage evident at the very start of the Southern Song than the Jingkang Incident (*Jingkang shibian* 靖康事變), so named for the ephemeral reign period of the emperor Qinzong 欽宗 (r. 1126), which of course precipitated the establishment of the dynasty as such.

The first full-fledged mobilization of Jurchen Jin forces against the Song dynastic state culminated in 1125, and it was arguably the ironic result of the military ineptitude of the latter. After many decades of domination by the stronger confederation of the Kitan (also Khitan or, in Chinese, Qidan 契丹) Liao dynasty (907–1125) (Wittfogel and Fêng, 1949; Standen, 2007),[27] the Jurchen people had risen in revolt in 1114, declaring their new Jin dynasty in the course of the following year, 1115. Seeking to forge an alliance against their long-standing overlords, these Jurchen tribesmen solicited and procured the aid of the Song Chinese in mobilizing against their Kitan oppressors. Resulting from centuries of conflict with the Kitan dating back as far as early Tang times (Yang, 2022: 48), the Chinese were likely already well disposed, if not incentivized, to ally themselves with the Jurchen. Nonetheless, as an added enticement, the Jin promised the Song the return of sixteen northernmost prefectures, commonly referred to as the "sixteen prefectures of Yan and Yun" (Yan Yun

---

[26] The semi-agrarian Jurchen people, as Tungusic-speaking natives of what today is Manchuria, were the ancestors of the people who became later known as the Manchus, who would establish their own Qing dynasty (1644–1911) as the last of the imperial orders in China.

[27] The para-Mongolic Kitan people were descended from proto-Mongols, with their language having admixtures of Turkic (Uyghur) and Koreanic elements, and their dynastic territory incorporating extensive portions of present-day southern Siberia and northeastern China. Despite being nomadic and initially hostile, the Kitan certainly became over time among the more overtly Sinicized or "Chinese-like" of the groups with which the Song had dealings, with ethnic Han inhabitants eventually comprising a substantial portion of their population.

shiliu zhou 燕雲十六州), which had come under control of the Liao in 938
(Mote, 1999: 64–65, 195, 208). However, following a series of surprisingly
swift victories against their former dominators, in which their incompetent Song
Chinese allies played no appreciable role, the Jin saw no reason to maintain this
unproductive alliance. Thus, the pact, which had taken nearly eight years to
finalize, quickly eroded, dissolving completely by mid-1123, at which point,
with the ultimate defeat of the Liao well in hand, the Jin began redirecting their
attacks incrementally against their former partner, the Song.

This first of these Jin–Song wars, initiating a series of armed conflicts
occurring between roughly 1123 and 1126, began with largely unsuccessful
strikes against northern Chinese cities such as Taiyuan 太原 (in modern Shanxi
山西 province) (Tao, 1977: 21). However, incrementally, the endemic offensive
soon became mortally consequential with the targeting of the central heartland
of the empire and the walled capital of Bianjing 汴京 – destined ultimately to be
known exclusively as Kaifeng 開封 (in today's Henan 河南 province) – itself
(Levine, 2009: 628–33). It appears that the Jin had become increasingly intent
on exacting the ultimate penalty on the Song dynasty, not only because of its
military ineptitude against the Liao but also because of its seemingly inexhaust-
ible wealth.

Eventually, as the Jurchen enemy bore down on Bianjing in late January of
1126, suddenly shocked by a reversal of fortune long in the making, the reigning
Song emperor Huizong 徽宗 (r. 1100–26) readied himself to flee south, at least
temporarily, in order to avoid capture, with the expectation of returning once the
danger had passed. However, arguing that imperial absence was tantamount to
capitulation, Huizong's advisers at court persuaded him that he could not simply
leave the Song state without a ruler at such a critical time. Consequently, just
prior to the sighting on the northern horizon of the leading Jin armies, Huizong
abdicated, undergoing the associated ritual ceremony (*neishan* 內禪) and retir-
ing as emperor in favor of his eldest son, Qinzong, who was destined to rule as
emperor merely from early 1126 until the fall of the capital at the end of the
Chinese lunar and turn of the Western solar calendar year. Huizong therewith
departed to more southerly turf, leaving his son and successor alone to face the
enemy. Qinzong managed to forestall the inevitable defeat of the Song by Jin
forces at that time by consenting to the payment of the colossal annual indemnity the invaders demanded (Franke, 1994: 229; Lorge, 2005: 52–53).[28]

---

[28] Being the equal to about 180 years' worth of the tribute previously paid to the Jin each year since
1123, the demanded indemnity per annum consisted of "50 million taels of silver, 5 million taels
of gold, 1 million packs of silk, 1 million packs of satin, 10,000 horses, 10,000 mules, 10,000
cattle, and 1,000 camels." A tael is a Chinese weight measurement of about 1.3 Western ounces
or about forty grams.

However, upon the withdrawal of Jin forces after the conclusion of negotiations, Qinzong, in short order, reneged on the deal and, to the future detriment of the capital itself, provocatively but without an intelligible strategy, positioned troops out in the prefectural cities to serve as a diffuse and ill-defined buffer against any impending Jurchen encroachments (Lorge, 2005: 53).

As a result, by December of 1126, embittered to the hilt by these continuing acts of duplicity, the former Jurchen ally-turned-enemy returned to Chinese soil with the punitive determination of following up in full on the prior assault of less than a year earlier and, on 9 January 1127, despite staunch resistance, Bianjing finally fell to these invading Jin forces (Tao, 1977: 21). Thereupon, the reigning emperor Qinzong, having ruled for merely a year, and his father Huizong, who was detained this time in the midst of another southward flight, were both captured and taken as prisoners by the Jin army. The Jurchen invaders' tactic of taking the living person of the ruler hostage mirrored ancient Chinese convention. Logically, whenever possible in wartime, a premium was placed on taking defeated monarchs alive, as opposed either to killing them outright or permitting them the opportunity to kill themselves before capture, such that it came to be considered normative operative procedure, as a way of either imposing or reinforcing the vassalage of a conquered state. What had often ensued in the past was that the captured and held oppositional king was eventually ransomed back at great cost, with this practice being rooted in China's oldest political foundations, datable in fact as far back as to the transition from the Shang to the Zhou dynasty (Holcombe, 2011: 31; Major and Cook, 2017: 90, 98, 105).[29] Ransoming was to desist in practice under non-Chinese regimes. Moreover, whereas the seizure of a single sovereign by an enemy was hardly unprecedented in Chinese history, this simultaneous capturing of *two* of the most vaunted human symbols of Chinese authority – the immediate past ruler as well as his successor – by the alien Jurchen forces certainly was unique and doubtless was viewed as doubly advantageous to their purposes.

Similarly, while it had also occurred in the past and was destined to recur in the future, the act of imperial abdication, which required the ritual demotion of the sitting ruler to retired status in order to elevate a new emperor, was also quite uncustomary in China. Moreover, especially in this instance, with hindsight, we can discern that Huizong's ceding of his investiture to Qinzong likely had some bearing on the subtle but detectable differences in how each man has been

---

[29] The earliest such instance remains perhaps the most famous. It involves the reputed seven years of captivity as a hostage in the hands of the Shang of the illustrious King Wen (Wen Wang 文王; born as Ji Chang 姬昌; died in 1050 BCE), the third ruler of the Zhou as a people and the nominal founder of their dynasty. Vengeance sought for this indignity is thought in part to have driven the Zhou people to overthrow the Shang.

perceived in history, if not by their Jurchen captors, who seem to have heaped humiliation on them both equally. Qinzong's insertion as a kind of placeholder at least partially accounts for why traditional historians have tended to view his rule as fictive in comparison to that of his father Huizong, with the latter being regarded as having been more legitimate and, to a certain degree, even iconic. Qinzong's reign, its brevity notwithstanding, is regarded as neither of these. According to protocol, upon his ascension, Qinzong, even as a son, became positioned above his former emperor of a father in rank. Yet, neither in the minds of posterity nor in the eyes of their Jurchen captors of the time did this reversal seem to hold. As historian Patricia Buckley Ebrey has observed, once he became emperor, Qinzong, at least technically, outranked Huizong, with the retired emperor thereupon expected to obey the directives of his son. However, she further notes that, upon becoming hostages of the Jin, "Huizong's seniority in the family structure seems to have taken precedence over their recent political rank and most authorities treat Huizong as the head of any group of captives that included him" (Ebrey, 2014: 501).

A reconstituted namesake version of the Song, called in subsequent history the Southern Song because of the constricted geography it was forced to accept, was to continue improbably, with diminished military prowess but previously unequalled economic prosperity until 1279 (Holcombe, 2011: 130–31). Nonetheless, with this anticlimactic removal of its leadership as just described, the original or "Northern" Song dynasty arrived at a sudden and ignominious end. However, most pertinent to our present set of concerns is that this fateful occasion, resulting in the decapitation of governance, also marks the beginning of the infamous episode known as the Shame, Disgrace, Calamity, or Humiliation of Jingkang (*Jingkang zhi chi* 靖康之恥), named as it was for the star-crossed reign of Qinzong – and which almost cruelly may be translated as "pacified well-being" (*jingkang* 靖康). As we shall see, in nearly every conceivable way, any and all of these dispiriting designations for what took place are entirely apt.

On March 20, 1127, the occupying Jurchen forces at Bianjing summoned forth the captive emperors Qinzong and Huizong to present them with the directive received from their own then-reigning, second Jin ruler, Taizong 太宗 (Wuqimai 吳乞買; r. 1123–35). According to the directive, the two former rulers of the extinguished Song state, having already been held prisoner for over two months, were to be reduced to commoner status, deprived of all ceremonial trappings, and forced to endure the plundering and requisitioning of the imperial palace for use as a command compound for occupying enemy troops (Franke, 1994: 233–34; Mote, 1999: 197; Levine, 2009: 642–43). This announcement, moreover, heralded the torturous weeks that were to follow of wholesale brutalization of the Song populace at the hands of the Jin. This unrestrained brutality included looting, arson, rape, and the enslavement of those prisoners of war who had not been already summarily executed.

The materials that document the atrocities that unfolded at Bianjing and radiated across North China beginning in 1127 are scarce. However, as an extant source now available for our scrutiny that exposes the tragic intricacies and intimacies of the Jingkang Incident, despite being a product of the immediately succeeding Southern Song era, nothing surpasses the compilation *The Accounts of Jingkang* (*Jingkang baishi jianzheng* 靖康稗史箋證), or also *Seven Accounts of Jingkang* (*Jingkang baishi qizhong* 靖康稗史七种).[30] Constituting a composite work, *Accounts of Jingkang* consists of seven discrete and relatively brief records by an assortment of authors either contemporary or nearly so with the cataclysmic event, some of whom are known to us, and others who are destined to remain forever anonymous. Nevertheless, the common thread linking them all is the fact that each author survived the abrupt shift into the Southern Song era and preponderantly matured during it. Consequently, this collection provides us with a most thoroughgoing and extensively circumspective record of the excesses that transpired during the Jingkang crisis. Therefore, being at once an eminently dispassionate but oftentimes disturbingly graphic collage of what actually occurred during this transitional and transformative historical moment, *Accounts of Jingkang* is, by every objective measure, a uniquely informative document.

This is not to say, however, that it is an objective corpus. Although its various authors vary in their restraint or expressiveness, we nonetheless find retrospectively coursing throughout *Accounts of Jingkang* a palpable dismay about the dilemma of survival confronted by the once ostensibly sovereign Song state. Together with this dispiriting malaise, one also detects in the writing undercurrents of shock and outrage that this disgraceful brutalization of the Chinese population and, most of all, its monarchy, for the first time in historical memory on such a grand scale, had been rapaciously inflicted by upstart foreigners who previously had been held fairly comfortably at bay, even if largely through their domination by a more customary and familiar, if similarly detested, enemy in the form of the Kitan (Davis, 1996: 152–53).

Depending on the voice and the agenda of the given author, the notices that stock *Accounts of Jingkang* are sometimes chronicle-like and quasi-journalistic,

---

[30] The seven distinct texts are: (1) *Xuanhe yiyi fengshi Jinguo xing chenglu* 宣和乙巳奉使金國行程錄 [Tour of Duty to the State of Jin from 1119 to 1125]; (2) *Wengzhong ren yu* 甕中人語 [Utterances of a Man in a Jar]; (3) *Kaifeng fu zhuang* 開封府狀 [Circumstances in Kaifeng Prefecture]; (4) *Nanzheng luhui* 南征錄彙 [Expedition to the South]; (5) *Qinggong yiyu* 青宮譯語 [Transmissions from the Green Palace]; (6) *Shenyin yu* 呻吟語 [Moaning]; and (7) *Songfu ji* 宋俘記 [Records of Song Captives].

even matter-of-fact in their straightforwardness. At other times, they are imbued with wrenching emotiveness. However, at least in my view, what emerges as most strikingly consistent from any scholarly reading and analysis of this record of its namesake event is just how normative an expectation it was that especially the *women* of the former Song court would be and were subjected to the brunt of imposed enslavement. These generally elite women, irrespective of what social rank they had enjoyed prior to the invasion, defeat, and occupation of Bianjing by the Jin, were routinely and almost indiscriminately relegated to the effective status of slaves through forced marriages, forcibly having to enter into relationships of concubinage with their Jurchen captors, and simply by being sold into sexual servitude. Although their male counterparts were also enslaved, the reality is that the all-too-common lot of these subjugated women informs us far better regarding the violent nexus of war and unfreedom that prevailed during the most crucial centuries of the Chinese midimperial age.

We quickly learn from *Accounts of Jingkang*, as well as other sources of comparable vintage and later, that many, if not most, of these Chinese court women of the doomed Song dynasty did not readily or willingly submit to a fate of abject enslavement. Indeed, we can infer that so unnerving was these women's dread of life spent in captivity at the utter mercy of a barbarous Jurchen warrior that they instead elected to kill themselves in droves. Drowning, in particular, appears in the sources as a method of escape into death much preferred over others. Or, as military historian of China, Peter Lorge has prosaically and succinctly stated the matter, "Many palace women drowned themselves rather than be given to the Jurchen invaders" (Lorge, 2005: 54).[31]

Moreover, from *Accounts of Jingkang*, we learn straightaway that these women of the court frequently had good reason for resorting to suicide. The Jurchen adversary meted out unspeakable brutality for even the slightest resistance exercised by these captive women. As evidence, we need only take into account the cautionary example of the three mistresses Zhang, Lu, and Cao, for we are informed that:

> Maiden martyrs Mistresses Zhang, Lu, and Cao resisted the Second [Jin] Prince's advances, for which he had them impaled with iron rods and placed in front of a tent where they were left to bleed to death over three days. On the seventh day of the [first] month, the imperial consorts and the other concubines entered the stockade. Whereupon, the prince pointed to the example of the corpses of Zhang, Lu, and Cao as a warning against resistance, and the consorts and concubines thereupon all begged for their lives.
>
> (Nai'an, 1994[?]: 4.5)

---

[31] See also Davis, 1996: 116; Ebrey, 2014: 468.

The savage cruelty with which the three ladies Zhang, Lu, and Cao were dispatched, however, provides us with much more than just another in the long line of examples of the Jurchen penchant for impaling as the favored form of execution. It also apprises us of the enigmatic nature yet predictable manner of the Jurchen willfulness in asserting power over those subjugated, serving to show just how suddenly the apperception of any resistance by those at their mercy could almost instantly convert into murderously sadistic and uncontained rage.

Nevertheless, we also discover that many other courtly women were left without the alternative of ending it all, even if they had initially been disposed toward doing so. An especially conspicuous example of someone prominent who had this opportunity snatched away, even if she was inclined to pursue it, is supplied by Zhao Fujin 趙富金, the daughter of the former emperor Huizong himself. We learn that, despite her having been another man's wife, after becoming a captive upon the fall of Bianjing, she was wedded to a Jurchen prince. We are informed that during his journey back north, Sheyema 設野馬 or 設也馬 (also Sheyemu 設野母) lusted after Zhao Fujin and took her as a wife along the way (Nai'an, 1994[?]: 4.6). After he had returned with her to (the principal Jin capital of) Shangjing 上京 (literally, "Supreme Capital"; the modern Harbin 哈尔滨 in Manchuria), Taizong decreed by edict that "the Imperial Concubine Zhao Fujin as well as the Concubines Xu Shengying, Yang Diao'er, and Chen Wenwan were all to be bestowed as wives upon Sheyema" 賜帝姬趙富金、王妃徐聖英、宮嬪楊調兒、陳文婉侍設野馬郎君爲妻 (Nai'an, 1994[?]: 5.3, 6.4).

Their Jurchen captors deliberately conceived of the Chinese abductees' journey north in their clutches as the ultimate and final indignity to be exacted upon the Song, and appreciating it as such is as significant for our understanding now as it was fateful for the historical actors then. Having secured Bianjing fully by the spring of 1127, the Jurchen forces thereupon methodically resolved to translocate all of the Song courtiers that they held captive, transporting them by means of what is described as seven large convoys northward, principally to Shangjing, the foremost among the several otherwise directional capitals of the Jurchen homeland (Mote, 1999: 197). This action of transporting their captive imperial clansmen as deeply as possible into what is now modern Manchuria was part of the Jurchen master plan of snuffing out all vestiges of the Song state. Transferal into the distant northern hinterland was intentionally designed to extirpate physically all human sources that might serve as potential rallying points for future resistance, because it appears the Jin captors constantly anticipated attack by loyalist Song forces dispatched to rescue the captive sovereigns.

We may cite *Accounts of Jingkang* as being among the sources indicating that, at least at the start, these Song captives transported by the Jin numbered nearly 15,000 persons (Ebrey, 2014: 476, 478). We also learn of the stark disparity in the overall survival rates between men and women, strongly suggesting that the latter were generally far more coveted than the former as captives:

> In the orderly procession northward to the border were 14,000 people, separated into different routes and times of departure. As for those who reached [the sixteen prefectures of] Yan and Yun, men survived at a rate of 40 percent and women at a rate of 70 percent. As for who survived and who perished, with it being unclear, we can know nothing further about it in order to trace their identities. (Nai'an, 1994[?]: 7.1a–b)

Given what it will come to suggest about differences in appraised worth, we should bear this gaping disparity in survival rates in mind.

Yet, despite this attested imprecision in identifying who it was among the captives overall who lived or died, we do find that *Accounts of Jingkang* unequivocally informs us in substantial detail about the attrition incurred from the harshness of the ordeal experienced by the very first and most prized of these transferals:

> The lead group, composed of imperial family members and relatives, contained more than 2,200 males and 3,400 females and departed on the 27th day of the third month of 1127 from the Qingcheng Stockade. When it arrived in Yanshan [today's Fangshan 房山, a southwestern district of Beijing 北京] on the 27th day of the following month, just over 1,900 females remained; as for the number of males, it lacks investigation. (Nai'an, 1994[?]: 7.1b)

Thus, the arduousness of the trek itself dictated that many would perish along the way, resulting in staggering rates of mortality. In truth, regarding this first of the convoys, comprised largely of the imperial family and clansmen, Ebrey, in interpreting corroborating traditional sources, states that "because of the long journey, exposure to the elements and inadequate food, many had perished, and women and children unable to ride horses had been abandoned on the road, so that less than 3,000 had reached Yanjing; moreover, in the next couple of weeks about half of them died" (Ebrey, 2014: 486–87).

In my view, this forced march north of these Song Chinese captives is significant also because it functions as a crucial definitional determinant. Through it, we can arrive at a fully tenable determination of the utter indistinguishability of slave status from what we might otherwise categorize as nothing more than that of being a prisoner of war. While we can rather facilely acknowledge intellectually that these two statuses need not necessarily be mutually exclusive, in the context of the events stemming from the Jingkang Incident, we can construe this equivalency quite palpably. Moreover, beyond this revelation, we can intuit that it was no less the coming of the Song captives under Jurchen control than it was their physical translocation within Jurchen territory that made them fully "commodifiable" or "commoditizable" as slaves. As historian Jing-shen Tao classically apprises us, among the Jurchen tribes, the capture of civilians as prisoners of war had long been a particularly favored and effectively institutionalized way of acquiring such slaves, with the practice of slavery itself becoming installed as an institutional bedrock (Tao, 1977: 18, 28, 29, 56, 74–75, 77, 96). Referring conceivably as far back as the early tenth century, with the initiation of contact between them through the exchange of tribute, according to Tao, "Slavery had its origin in earlier times, when the Jurchen captured the Chinese when they invaded North China, and … moved many Chinese from there to Manchuria as slaves" (Tao, 1977: 50–51).[32] Furthermore, as Tao observes, "The Jurchen, in unifying all the clans and conquering other peoples, used prisoners of war as the slave class" (Tao, 1977: 11).

The abundantly protean *Accounts of Jingkang* further informs us that, once ensconced in the Jurchen lands of Yanjing 燕京 (the present Beijing) and northward, "seized men of the Song were sold into slavery to the [Tangut] state of Xia, in exchange for horses, at a ratio of ten men for one horse" 所掠宋人,至夏國易馬,以 十易一 (Nai'an, 1994[?]: 6.7b).[33] Women, especially former Song princesses, were confined to a portion of the Jin palace, referred to possibly euphemistically as the Laundry Hall (*huanyi yuan* 浣衣院) (Nai'an, 1994[?]: 6.11, 6.12, 7.4b, 7.5b– 6b).[34] There, if not forced to perform as prostitutes, they were publicly auctioned. We learn that, "for only eight pieces of gold, one purchaser acquired a songstress who was discovered to have been a prince's granddaughter, prime minister's daughter-in-law, and a degree-holding civil official's wife" 以八金買倡婦,賣爲 亲王女孫、相國侄婦、進士夫人 (Nai'an, 1994[?]: 6.2b). Thus, if one is at all objective, then one is surely challenged not to regard the unfortunates in such circumstances as those described by *Accounts of Jingkang* as anything other than slaves. Such an acknowledgment also assists us in appreciating why this tragic event has continued to exert a profoundly anguishing influence on the Chinese cultural psyche even into modern times.

Despite its indisputable thoroughness and effective success in seeking to bring about the termination of the original Song dynastic state through the capture and abduction of its imperial house, the Jurchen Jin nonetheless failed

---

[32] The first reference to the Jurchen people in Chinese sources appears in 748. See (Elliott, 2001: 47–48).

[33] See Ebrey, 2014: 495. The dynastic state of Xia 夏, which was referred to by the exonym Xi Xia 西夏 or Western Xia by the Chinese, was that of the proto-Tibeto-Burman Tangut (in Chinese, Dangxiang 黨項) people. It existed from 1038 to 1227, until its defeat and the liquidation of its population by the Mongols.

[34] See also Ebrey, 2006: 16; Ebrey, 2014: 493, 497.

to obliterate Song leadership completely. In an ironic way, the captive emperor-patriarch Huizong was to succeed ultimately through his prolificacy. Of his twenty-six living sons in 1127 – he had actually fathered thirty-one[35] – all but one had been captured during the Jingkang Incident (Ebrey, 2014: 498–99). This lone escapee, Zhao Gou 趙構 (1107–87), was destined eventually to become Gaozong 高宗 (r. 1127–62) and, after many harrowing near-captures by relentless Jurchen pursuers over many years, he would go on to establish the Southern Song dynasty at Lin'an 臨安 (the future Hangzhou 杭州 of modern Zhejiang 浙江 province). From there, in the interim between his father's death in Jurchen captivity in 1135 and his elder brother's continued languishing in the same until death in 1161, Gaozong would sign the Treaty of Shaoxing (*Shaoxing heyi* 紹興和議) with the Jin in 1141. In doing so, he thereby ceded to the occupying alien dynasty territorial control of all of China north of the Huai 淮 River, and thus formally acknowledged the de facto situation as it had already existed for nearly fifteen years.[36]

However, as hardly the first of the dynasties formed by non-Chinese to threaten the enduring empire of the Chinese existentially and even to claim partial and temporary control over it, the Jin certainly would not be the last. As fate would have it, however traumatizing it might have been at that time, the Jurchen role as tormenting enslavers of the Chinese was not to endure long beyond the Jingkang Incident, and assuredly did not extend very much geographically south of the northern territories of their domain. Over time, within the course of several decades, the customarily persistent forces of Sinicization – or, to offer its more contemporary equivalent, "Hanicization" – consistently, if never completely, countervailed ongoing Chinese enslavement, as the estranging factor of otherness distinguishing Han and Jurchen became increasingly attenuated via such mitigating factors as voluntary intermarriage (Tao, 1977: ix, 28, 29, 95–98). We could further note a range of clear concessions made by the occupiers to the occupied, such as the Jurchen adoption of Chinese surnames. However, these Sinicizing trends notwithstanding, in just over a century following the traumatizing events at Bianjing, whatever lingering potentiality for further victimization of the Chinese by the Jurchen occupation was eradicated altogether, as the familiar dynastic cycle inexorably progressed, and the Jin dynasty met its own totalistic destruction and extinction at the hands of a newly

---

[35] See Mote, 1999: 291. Huizong is known to have produced more offspring – sixty-five, during his time as reigning monarch – than any other emperor in Chinese history. See Ebrey, 2014: 301–11.

[36] Ratified by the arrival of a Jurchen envoy in 1142, the treaty is named for the city of Shaoxing, in eastern Zhejiang, where it was finalized. In addition to the cession of territory and other provisions, the Southern Song became responsible for the paying of tribute to the Jin, in the form of a quarter-million taels of silver and bolts of silk annually until 1164. See Tao, 1977: 68, 87, 88; Franke, 1994: 234; Mote, 1999: 298; Beckwith, 2009 [repr. 2011]: 175).

emerged, mortally menacing power. The wholesale destruction of the Jin dynasty of North China was achieved by the Mongols (in Chinese, Menggu 蒙古), who – after becoming molded into a cohesive confederation out of what were once Mongolic culturo-linguistically related but mutually antagonistic tribes – began to assert their dominance on the world stage under their unifier Chinggis [or Genghis] Khan (ca. 1162–1227).[37]

Once consolidated into a unified people under the leadership of Chinggis in 1206, the Mongols were driven to mobilize against the Jurchen Jin dynasty for a welter of reasons. Among others, medieval historian Peter Jackson notes that well before the emergence of Chinggis, the Jin regime was already known to the Mongols as an ally of an adversary – namely, the neighboring Tatar tribal confederation of eastern Mongolia, which had in fact been responsible for the murder of Chinggis' father, Yesügei, in about the year 1170 (Jackson, 2017: 63). Consequently, premised on the converse dictum that the "friend of my enemy is my enemy," from the very outset, based on its affinity with the Tatars, the Mongols felt they had direct enough cause for vengeance against the Jin. We can also simply observe that once Chinggis had risen to paramountcy as Great Khan and set his ambitions on plundering the renowned "land of riches" that was China, achieving that goal logistically required the removal of the Jin (Mote, 1999: 410). Consequently, we can plainly see that, all things considered, the chief transgression of the Jin as well as its Tatar allies was that of having foolishly interposed themselves between the Mongols and the enormous and irresistible wealth of China, which was their principal object of desire, just as it had been for their invading Jurchen forerunners.

However, beyond these transparent geopolitical impetuses, especially in light of our present concerns, we may also include a more socioeconomically exploitive factor as doubtless spurring Mongol antipathy toward the Jurchen-led dynasty. Although least recognized and therefore largely overlooked, this factor is precisely that of a predatory history of enslavement. As we have seen, *Accounts of Jingkang* oftentimes furnishes many incidental revelations and, in this instance, we find that it reliably confirms that, as much as a century before mortal combat against the Jin empire was to ensue, Mongol males already occupied a prescribed place and valuation in the Jurchen institutionalized taxonomy of slavery, for it is written that: "Moreover, Koreans and Mongols were sold into slavery for two pieces of gold each" 又賣高麗蒙古爲奴人，二金 (Nai'an, 1994[?]: 6.7b). No doubt, even if not for the Koreans, for the Mongols, especially once they were eminently empowered to redress it, such a past affront

---

[37] For more on the obscurity of Mongol origins and the unlikeliness of their emergence as the preeminently dominating military force that they became, see Mote, 1999: 8, 34, 81, 140, 403–10.

committed against them by the Jin state as the routine consignment of their captured men categorically to slave status served as a potent stimulus to settling a long-held grievance – that is, once and for all. As a result, for what must have been an untold complex of reasons, within which enmity over enslavement is sure to have figured in the mix, in a protracted series of attacks spanning the two-plus decades from 1212 to 1234, the Mongols obliterated the Jin dynasty beyond any discernible indication that it had ever existed (Mote, 1999: 248).

This example of the thoroughness of the Mongol erasure of the Jurchen Jin dynasty and decimation of its people notwithstanding, of those victims of their incursions who secured their own survival through the deprecating gesture of immediate and unconditional surrender, the Mongols were notorious enslavers. Operating in conformance with what Peter Jackson has further described as the "laws of war," any city that compliantly submitted was spared, whereas any city that resisted and required subjugation by force was subjected to "a general massacre, at least of the menfolk, while the females were enslaved" (Jackson, 2017: 163). However, we should be mindful that life itself as a non-Mongol under Mongol dominion connoted always tacitly occupying enslaved status. Even those above the commoner classes, including the largely Turkic allies of the Mongols, were theoretically never at a great remove from enslavement and were, as frequently as became necessary, reminded of it.

Let us finally note that, in a manner analogous with the Jurchen predilections that were so salaciously evinced in the case of the Jingkang Incident, Mongol practices in slavery also would eventually incorporate a quite conspicuous trade in women, although it would differ by not involving the women of conquered China but instead those of the subdued neighboring state of Korea (Biran, 2021: 84). Conforming to earlier Chinese norms, this pursuit involved the fetishistic desire that arose among Mongol men for the procurement of Korean women and girls. This fetishism originally took root in official circles, in connection with the tribute relations, especially after 1280, that the Yuan imperial court conducted with the Goryeo dynasty (Wyatt, 2022: 117–20). Having been cowed into submission two full decades before the Yuan dynastic founding in 1279, Korea had become a formal but still technically semi-autonomous vassal state of China by 1270 (Pratt, 2006: 102–4). It would remain as such up until 1356, merely a dozen years before the overthrow and expulsion of the Mongols. As the reigning emperor at the time that tribute relations commenced, Khubilai Khan [also Qubilai Qan or Qubilai Qaghan] (1215–94; r. 1260–94), the ablest of the many grandsons of Chinggis and the khan presiding over that easternmost subdivision of the Mongol Empire comprising China, probably had as much to do with perpetuating, if not initiating, the avid pursuit of Korean females as any other factor.

In the year 1259, when the Korean crown prince was en route to the Yuan capital of Cambaluc (also Khanbaliq or Dadu [or Daidu] 大都; the future Beijing), he chanced to meet his counterpart Khubilai in the field. Rightly regarding him as the de facto ruler and soon-to-be khan of China, the Korean prince pledged fealty to him. Khubilai, for his part, accepted the humble submission of the visiting prince and gave him one of his own daughters in marriage (Henthorn, 1971 [repr. 1974]: 120; Lee, 1997: 72). Thereafter, Khubilai enthusiastically endorsed and encouraged intermarriage between Mongols and Koreans. However, as we might expect, over time, especially below the level of the court, many of the unions that ensued fell far short of the ideals connoted by marriage, with Korean women being privately and oftentimes pruriently purchased by Mongol as well as allied West Asian (mainly Turkic) retainers to serve out their days as concubines, servants, and slaves.

Given the evidence suggested by records datable to as early as the third century before the Common Era, we can surmise that elite Chinese men had actually preceded the Mongols in a professed preference for Korean women (Holcombe, 2011: 79–81). Moreover, entries in later official histories, such as those of the Tang dynasty, explicitly confirm how Korean women were frequently dispatched to the Chinese imperial court as gifts of tribute (Wilbur, 1943 [repr. 2016]: 92–93; Schafer, 1963: 44). However, by the time of the Mongols, especially revealing in this connection is that at least a few extant literary corpora written by Chinese authors living under the Yuan dynasty (1279–1368) overtly describe either captivation with the attractiveness of Korean women, a fixation that they of course shared, or else the obsessive avidness with which the Mongol conquerors were intent on procuring these women for themselves. Reifying the former trend is a comment offered by the envoy Hao Jing 郝經 (1223–75), who with clear luridness refers to what appears to have been the generally held consensus regarding Korean women as having "flesh like jade snow emitting clouds and mists" 肌膚玉雪發雲霧 (Hao, 1983: 10.21).[38] Another comment supplied by the philosopher Ye Ziqi 葉子奇 (ca. 1327–after 1390) attests not only to the foregoing ideation but also to the fact that, despite possessing a generalizable beauty that had situated many of them as members with status of the Yuan court, untold numbers of Korean women once in China were instead relegated to lives of subjugated servitude. As Ye states the matter: "As for northerners, for maids, they must get [Korean] (Gaoli) women and girls . . . . If it is otherwise, then they are said not to be

---

[38] "Clouds and mists" (*yunlu* 雲霧) or "clouds and rain" (*yunyu* 雲雨) is an age-old and commonplace poetic allusion to physical love or simply fornication. See McNaughton, 1971: 51–52.

deserving of becoming officials" 北人, 女使, 必得高麗女孩童 … 不如此,謂
之不成仕宦 (Ye, 1959: 3B.63).

Ye Ziqi's comment became available in writing no earlier than 1378, when
the Yuan dynasty had – a decade earlier – given way to the Ming dynasty (1368–
1644) and the restoration of native rule. With his life having spanned the
transition between dynasties, the contents of his book *Caomuzi* 草木子
(*Master of Grasses and Trees*) unsurprisingly consists of a discursive mixture
of historical commentary on both periods. Consequently, we cannot know with
complete confidence whether the "northerners" he refers to above were ethnically Mongol or Han. Nevertheless, even the supposition that the "northerners"
Ye Ziqi refers to were likely his fellow Chinese neither discounts nor discredits
the possibility that this described insistency on procuring Korean women had
become by Ming times a vestige practice. In sum, whether perceived as
a heritable legacy extension of that same documented practice of the Mongol
conquerors of the immediately preceding era or not, the preponderance of his
life spent under Yuan rather than Ming dominion itself makes Ye's reference to
"northerners" just as likely a signifier for the Mongols and their mainly Turkic
allies in China as not.

From the foregoing deliberations on what transpired in the arena of human
bondage in China from the inception of Southern Song through and beyond
Yuan times, essentially from the twelfth century of the Common Era until the
mid-fourteenth, we arguably extract at least three distinct but related sets of
rewardingly edifying lessons. The first of these sets fittingly adumbrates the
theme with which our deliberations began, for it is nothing other than the
enduringly interlocked nature of the relationship between war and slavery. If
nothing else, through our transversal but interlinked consideration of the infamous Jingkang Incident of 1127 and the extension of Mongol domination into and
over China, beyond our unavoidable realization that the chief driver of conflict
was always greed, we have learned something of just how much war functioned
as a peculiarly pernicious facilitator of unfreedom. In both instances, those of
the Jurchen and the Mongol invasions of China, respectively, both of which may
be regarded as case studies of sorts, we have been able to amply observe how,
unlike heritable slavery, war served as the vector that, with freakishly random
frequency, imposed unfreedom on individuals who were once free.

Admittedly, albeit compelling and convincing, one may tenably argue that this
first set of insights, in which war begets slavery, was after all to be anticipated.
However, even if such is the case, then – for me, at least – the second set really is
unforeseen. In China, during its turbulent midimperial centuries, there can be no
question that, just as was true nearly everywhere else in the world of that time,
whatever interstate strife and conflict that did prevail was fomented principally by

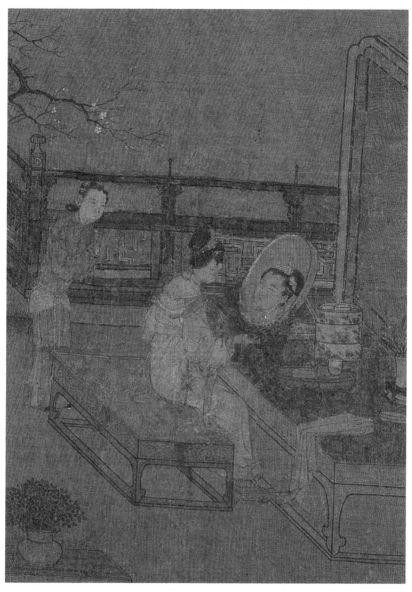

Figure 4 *Lady at Her Dressing Table in a Garden* (detail), by Su Hanchen, active 1120s–1160s. Museum of Fine Arts, Boston.

men. Most of all in medieval China, with its putative reputation of being perhaps the most archetypal among patriarchal social orders, one can argue persuasively that we should expect nothing otherwise. Consequently, most illuminating indeed is the salient discovery that the costs in terms of human liberty for whatever peace or normalization in interstate relations that was achieved seem to have fallen so much more heavily on women across this strife-ridden, war-torn period. Assuredly, as we have witnessed in the case of Jingkang and afterward as an episode, always possessing less agency and fewer recourses than their male counterparts, it was the women of the fallen Song and of vanquished Korea who were "made slaves" (*weinu* 爲奴) (See Figure 4).

Enslavement of Outsiders in Medieval East Asia: China's Inevitable African Slaves

Amidst the East Asian zone of medieval slavery, China was also the nearly exclusive terminal destination not only for foreign slaves of Asian origin but certainly those non-Asian slaves initially taken and enslaved from points well beyond the region. To be sure, in due course, these slaves brought to China from increasingly well outside the boundaries of the empire grew to include a kaleidoscopic panoply, with us being unlikely ever to account for all the places from which these peoples hailed. However, most important for our present pursuit is that, at some point in history that is still to be determined with precise exactitude, slaves originating from as distantly as continental Africa, almost invariably by transshipment, came to be regularly included within the steady infusion of captives into medieval China.

A truism of modern historical inquiry is that it affords ever-surprising revelations that force us to reexamine and continually revise our interpretations of the global past. One result of this enterprise has surely been the ongoing discovery that contact between widely dispersed and wholly unrelated peoples almost always seems to have occurred earlier than previously thought. However, when addressing the subject of the enslavement of Africans by non-Africans, we still somehow mentally resist situating slaves originating from Africa anywhere near a locale as physically and culturally remote as China.

The principle of geographical proximity logically compels us to regard any place much nearer to Africa than antipodean China as a far more viable point for contact and thus a more credible candidate for the dubious recognition as a bastion for the trading in African slaves. In addition to India, more likely "Asian" prospects are indeed the countries that anciently ringed the Persian Gulf as well as those that formed the populated zones of the Arabian Peninsula. Furthermore, our hunch is well confirmed by the fact that African slaves were at all times more numerous in the western portion of the Indian Ocean littoral zone than in its eastern portion (Campbell, 2008: 23). Over a period extending back some four millennia or more, the slave-trading inhabitants of these nearby territories pressed their advantage of being so close to an endless supply of

Africans who could be lured or captured and pressed into bondage (Campbell, 2008: 21). This observation also helps us in accounting for why conventions of transoceanic slave trafficking arose so much earlier on the eastern side of the African continent, where Muslim Arab merchants sought slaves as early as the eighth century CE and their Persian counterparts sought them even before then, than on the western side (Harris, 1971: 5–6; Parker, 2010 [repr. 2012]: 115).

This great geographical distance of China from the source of African slaves is not all that militates against Chinese involvement in their enslavement. A peculiar ethno-terminological puzzle also causes us to question the extent to which China ever did serve as a slaving venue for Africans. The earliest designation that the Chinese came to apply as an identifier for Africans was the term *kunlun* 崑崙 (Wyatt, 2010: 2–8). Kunlun as a descriptor for human beings is derived originally from a place-name, even as it inconveniently applies to a great number of places (Goodrich, 1931: 137–38). Still more problematically, Kunlun was the same name that the Chinese had already for centuries arbitrarily affixed to a profusion of non-African peoples, comprising Malays, Negritos, Papuans, Melanesians, Khmers, Champans, Srivijayans, Javanese, Borneans, Ceylonese, and Indians of South Asia as well as a host of West Asian (or Middle Eastern) peoples. The only qualification for Kunlun status was *relative* (that is, in comparison to the Chinese) darkness to black-ness of skin. This extremely low threshold qualified even the occasional Chinese as a Kunlun (Wyatt, 2010: 9, 15–16, 68–69; Wyatt, 2013 [repr. 2014]: 314–15; Yang, 2022: 53–54).

Consequently, ascertaining the geo-ethnicity of Kunlun referred to in the extant Chinese sources is challenging. Foremost among the difficulties is determining when a member of this designated catchall group subjected to enslavement in China was actually an African as opposed to being an inopportunely dark- or black-skinned member of one of these other groups. Indeed, based on the documentation available to us, ascertaining when the first Africans arrived as slaves in China in itself will always be a somewhat inexact exercise. On the one hand, from about the tenth or eleventh century CE onward, Chinese references to Kunlun may – more often than not – be persuasively interpreted as equivalent to references to Africans. Yet, on the other hand, complicating the endeavor are the many distinct Chinese names other than Kunlun – all of them disparaging – that had also emerged as designations for dark- to black-skinned individuals by this time (Filesi, 1972: 22). However, my objective here is less to offer a mere compendium of collective names that were commonplace at the time for these varied peoples than it is to demonstrate how a single name – that of Kunlun – was without question the main one used for the plausible as well as real African, regardless of specific time frame, throughout and even significantly beyond the medieval period. By extension, as we will see, the term progressively came to have an intimate and integral association with slavery.

As a reference to the black-bodied, if not to the enslaved, "Kunlun" appears in Chinese sources datable to the earliest centuries of the Common Era, and thus becomes prioritized in the inherited literature as a descriptor for such people, having early on attained classical status. Moreover, some modern authors suggest that included among even these very first of the historical Kunlun must indeed have been some Africans (Leur, 1955 [repr. 1967]: 99; Campbell, 2008: 21). This argument hinges on a claim that is difficult either to prove or disprove – namely, that mariners from Indonesian kingdoms such as Srivijaya and Java actually preceded the Arabs, if not the Persians, in their participation in the East African slave trade (Snow, 1988 [repr. 1989]: 17). This theory is additionally premised on the far less contentious idea that captives of African origin might well have entered China as slaves before the Chinese themselves had acquired a firm knowledge of the existence of Africa as a place. In the absence of either archaeological or written evidence, such a situation was nonetheless entirely possible. However, it remains for now unresolvable beyond all doubt. Therefore, with our interests better served in the pursuit of what we can know, let us cursorily consider the question of when it was that the Chinese first "discovered" Africa.

Based on the Chinese penchant for committing encounters with the exotic or unusual to writing, we are on safe ground in expecting the discovery of any African site to have achieved mention in a text. In this connection, albeit tenuous, some latter-day scholars have claimed to have found the first reference to Africa in a Chinese text in the *Weilue* 魏略 (*Brief History of Wei*), a work of the third century CE, attributed to the obscure author Yu Huan 魚豢, about whom nothing further is known (Filesi, 1972: 4, 18; Zhang, 1973: 2, 7, 9). Therein, "Africa" is arguably first referred to in the form of the isolated appearance of the name Wuchisan 烏遲散, which just might be the city of Alexandria in Egypt (Hirth, 1909: 46–47; Duyvendak, 1949: 8–9). Still, whether Wuchisan is truly identifiable with Alexandria remains debatable, and thus we find that we can neither reliably nor conclusively surmise that the Chinese had garnered any solid awareness of the existence of Africa before the ninth century CE.

Our much sought-after, first-ever reference in a Chinese source to an inarguably African territory would not appear for another six centuries. We must attribute it to Duan Chengshi 段成式 (ca. 803–63), an eccentric litterateur who lived during the Tang dynasty (Wyatt, 2010: 84–89). In his work *Youyang zazu* 酉陽雜俎 (*Miscellany of Tidbits from Youyang Mountain Cave*), Duan offers a singular description of Bobali 撥拔力, which scholars now concur to have been Berbera, or what is today the greater part of the northern coastline of the peninsular horn of modern Somalia (Wyatt, 2010: 84–87).

In customary Chinese fashion, before discussing its population, Duan Chengshi's description of Berbera begins with where he believes it to have been located, stating with at least vague accuracy: "The country of Bobali lies in the southwestern seas" 撥拔力國, 在西南海中 (Duyvendak, 1949: 13–14; Duan, 1975: 4.3b; Beachey, 1976a: 4; Beachey, 1976b: 1–2; Wyatt, 2010: 84–85). Yet, thereafter, inconclusiveness pervades Duan's unprecedented Africa entry especially in its description of the inhabitants of Berbera as Africans. He makes no mention of what then as well as now would have been the most fundamental distinguishing trait of the Berberans – that is, their darkness, indeed blackness, of skin color.

Even if it was not actually published until several centuries later, scholars believe that Duan Chengshi's miscellaneous compilation *Youyang zazu* was completed in approximately the year 855 (Filesi, 1972: 19; Wilkinson, 1973 [repr. 2015]: 741). Thereafter, we lack any explicit reference in a Chinese text either to Africa or to probable Africans for more than a century, when the mandate of rule over China had passed on to the succeeding Song dynasty. The reference itself is made only in passing and with such unremarkable soberness as to seem almost incidental, and yet we find that it has the unassailable distinction of appearing in an official source – the *Songshi* 宋史 (*History of the Song*). Of a Persian tribute delegation that arrived at the imperial court of the capital Kaifeng in order to commemorate the accession of the second ruler of the dynasty in the previous year, we are informed that:

> In 977, Envoy Pusina, Vice Commissioner Mohemo (Mahmud? Muhammad?), and Administrative Assistant Puluo and others made an offering of tribute [to the court] of the goods of their locality. Their servants, having deep-set eyes and black bodies, were called Kunlun slaves. By imperial decree, in return, these envoys were given suits of garments with lining, utensils, and currency; their servants were given variegated silk fabric, with differences [in each case]. (Tuotuo et al., 1977: 490.14118)

Were the Kunlun described here Africans? Although it is elliptically terse, the passage is unquestionably interlaced with the kinds of hints that encourage us to think so. The functioning of the slaves as "servants" of these emissaries of Persia does persuasively suggest that they had labored in such a capacity from the beginning of the trek and not been subdued and acquired somewhere intermediately, making their enslavement at some indeterminate juncture or junctures along the way seem unlikely. We also sense from this record the clear implication that, like the men behind whom they obediently trailed, these slaves would be returning to the place where they had all set out – that is, Persia. We may also assume that these slaves understood and received directives from their owners in Persian and neither in their own or one of the other multitudinous potential Kunlun languages. Thus, whereas these particular slaves cannot be deemed categorically to have been Africans, the extraction of slaves from Africa by Persian merchants that had been ongoing for ages surely encourages the attribution of an African identity to the Kunlun above described (Filesi, 1972: 24–25).

Apart from the salient entry describing the Persian tribute delegation of 977 just considered, we find that no official Chinese sources datable to the Song period refer again explicitly to the importation into China – either temporarily or permanently – of plausibly African slaves. However, in detailing events that occurred a century later, another *Songshi* entry not only reaffirms the requisite knowledge of Africa as a geographical entity on the part of the Chinese of that time but also provides us with vivid descriptions of their exposure to persons who were unmistakably Africans, even if they were not slaves. Through this latter set of entries, we actually learn of Africans traveling to China on two related occasions but receive no inkling that Chinese were as yet trekking to Africa. An account of the first of these eleventh-century encounters follows.

At a proximate but subsequent juncture in the *Songshi*, we find a somewhat detailed description of a country or perhaps a city called Cengtan 層檀, which appears to be a variant of Cengba 層拔, with both being names fairly common in Chinese parlance by the eleventh century for Zanzibar – meaning literally in Arabic the "Region of the Blacks," from south of the Juba River to Cape Delgado along the eastern coast of Africa (Wyatt, 2010: 69–70; Filesi, 1972: 2, 18, 20, 21). We further learn that:

> Cengtan is in the Southern Sea, with its town about twenty *li* (or seven miles) inland from the seacoast. In 1071, Cengtan brought gifts to our court for the first time. Traveling by sea, with the favorable [monsoon] winds, the envoy took 160 days. Sailing by way of Wuxun [in the vicinity of today's Muscat, Oman], Kollam [in India], and Palembang [in Indonesia], he arrived at Guangzhou. (Tuotuo et al., 1977: 490.14122)

Beyond its confirmation of a preference for travel to China by ship, which either may or may not be extended back to the previous instance of the Persian mission of 977, through the above description, we learn additional details about the locale called Cengtan. For instance, we are informed that the "language of its people sounds like that of the Arabs" 人語音如大食 and that it is "a land of warm winters and springs" 地春冬暖 (Tuotuo et al., 1977: 490.14122). Most important among these details, however, is that the initially nameless envoy of Cengtan becomes named: "In 1083, the envoy Protector Commandant Cengjiani 層伽尼 came [to China] again [bearing gifts] to court. [Our emperor] Shenzong 神宗 [r. 1067–85], recognizing the extreme distance he had traveled in returning, beyond presenting him with the same gifts as before, added 2,000 taels of silver" (Tuotuo et al., 1977: 490.14123).

We cannot know if the distinguished Cengjiani himself was black, or even if Cengtan in particular or Africa in general was his birthplace. Yet, even if he lacked African ancestry or provenance, we may be safely assured in believing Cengjiani to have come as directly as he could to China *from* Africa. Moreover, from the exaltedly prestigious title that the reigning Song emperor had bestowed on him, the latter half of which – "commandant" (*langjiang* 郎將) – was granted only occasionally to aboriginal chieftains of the borderland west and southwest, we can detect that the Chinese regarded this emissary from Africa with high esteem (Snow, 1988 [repr. 1989]: 20, 196).[39] However, most crucial for our purposes is that his name itself in Chinese (*ceng-jia-ni*) appears to be a phonetic approximation of the Arabicized Persian term *zanj* (also *zandj* or *zang* or *zeng*) or possibly the Latinized Arabic one *zinj*, which was likely meant also to denote his Zanzibarian place of origin (Filesi, 1972: 31; Dathorne, 1996: 74, 83, 164). Of course, given its literal meaning in Arabic as "the blacks," (Snow, 1988 [repr. 1989]: 9, 10; Dikötter, 1992 [repr. 2015: 9) we find that this same phoneticized corruption of the very term used by Arab traders for those they enslaved would eventually enter into and become a fixture of Chinese parlance as a designation for the increasing numbers of Africans they themselves would incrementally encounter.

Within three centuries of Duan Chengshi's initial and highly impressionistic description of Berbera, Chinese knowledge of Africa – either derived directly from dealings with first the Persians and subsequently with the Arabs themselves or channeled through mostly Chinese mariner go-betweens – had increased exponentially. Owing to hostile border relations especially during the latter part of the Song period, the Chinese found the customary Central Asian Silk Road land routes to be impassable. Therefore, whatever enhancement that did occur in what the Chinese knew geographically about Africa became an aspect of a still broader advancement in the acquisition of information about many other nearby and distant maritime states and their sundry peoples (Lo, 2012: 105).

Resulting at least in part from direct contact, Chinese awareness of the Zanj correspondingly increased and they gradually became identified more and more

---

[39] Snow refers to Cengjiani as "Zengjiani"; strictly proper pinyin transliteration dictates the former spelling.

closely with Africa itself as a location. However, we should be aware that this exposure was not always facilitated by either the Persian or Arab captors who were so familiar with the Zanj by lengthy historical association. Moreover, the fact that this trafficking in the Zanj was not exclusively in Persian and Arab hands reveals the surprising obliqueness of the varying means by which Africans evidently in the earliest centuries entered into Chinese captivity. Traditional Chinese sources on the Tang dynasty record the occasional delivery of Zanj captives as curiosities to the imperial court, with it being a phenomenon occurring as early as the eighth and ninth centuries. Contrary to what we might expect, however, more frequently than not, these records explicitly state that instead of being made by Persian or Arab emissaries, these sporadic deliveries of Zanj slaves were instead made by tribute missions dispatched to China from near-neighboring countries in the South China Sea. An excerpt extracted from an official entry in the *Xin Tangshu* 新唐書 (*New History of the Tang*) on the reception of the Javanese tribute delegation of 813 serves as a case in point, whereby we are informed that the emperor Xianzong 憲宗 (r. 806–20) "received four Zanj (*sengqi*) slaves, a five-colored parrot, human-faced birds, and the like" 獻僧祇奴四, 五色鸚鵡, 頻伽鳥等 (Ouyang, Song et al., 1976: 222C.6302).

On the one hand, the listing in this notice of these four enslaved Zanj unfortunates together with the exotic birds also delivered to the Chinese court unquestionably relegated them to something less than human, not only by the Javanese authorities who gifted them but also by the Chinese emperor and his entourage who received them. However, on the other hand, despite their vexing brevity, from this and similar accounts we learn with surety that the Zanj youths like these four who were periodically received at the Chinese court from afar were deemed in the estimation of imperial authority to be fully befitting of the category of marvels. We must regard the assignment of these Zanj slaves to this category as owing to a strangeness stemming from their unfamiliarity, which itself derives from what the Chinese already recognized as their having originated in a distant and irreducibly mysterious land.[40]

Toward the end of Song times in the twelfth and thirteenth centuries, written works on known and newly discovered overseas countries particularly flourished. The most famous of these books – *Lingwai daida* 嶺外代答 (*Information on the Lands South of the Wuling Mountains*) by Zhou Qufei 周去非 (*jinshi* 1163) and the aforementioned and earlier cited *Zhufan zhi* by Zhao Rugua, completed in 1178 and about 1225, respectively – include numerous treatises of

---

[40] Some impressionistic knowledge of the Zang among Chinese may well have also derived from their ninth-century revolt which shook the Muslim world to its core. See Phillips, 1985: 76–77.

varying length and detail on lands long familiar to as well as those being newly discovered by the Chinese (Wilkinson, 1973 [repr. 2015]: 760–61; Snow, 1988 [repr. 1989]: 11–14). These two works in particular shed detailed light on the different topographies, products, and peoples of East Africa. At that time, however, the Chinese still had only limited direct exposure to peoples from Africa, with what little that did occur being mediated chiefly through the Arab seamen who enslaved and traded in them. Consequently, Africans became increasingly known to the Chinese collectively as the Zanj, which was the name by which they were referred to by their Arab masters (Duyvendak, 1949: 23).[41] We should by no means overlook the biases that permeate and misinformation that lingers in these two books and the less comprehensive works that survive. Yet, despite their shortcomings, these revealing opuses of the twelfth and thirteenth centuries on the world beyond China greatly surpass in accuracy the mostly outlandish, ill-informed, and fantasy-riddled scribblings that preceded them (Lo, 2012: 105–6).

With the defeat and supplanting of the Song by the succeeding Yuan dynasty, China was subjected to foreign domination under the Mongols. The Yuan regime maintained an extensive network of foreign relations and, in the spirit of the Mongol drive for conquest and profit overall, encouraged the geographical study of the world. Still, our information on the eastward flow of Africans during Yuan times across what Chinese then called the Western Sea (that is, the Indian Ocean) is miniscule. On the one hand, this deficit in our knowledge about the seaborne movement of Africans into China under the Yuan is arguably in some measure attributable to the preoccupation of the Mongols as nomads mostly with their land-based empire, which caused them to fail to develop much beyond rudimentary skills as seafarers and led them also to minimize or even neglect nautical concerns. There is indeed much truth to the customary claim that the success of the Mongols in expanding and defending their acquired empire by sea was dismally deficient in comparison to that of their initial seizure of it on horseback (Wilkinson, 1973 [repr. 2015]: 777–78; Delgado, 2008: 168). On the other hand, the most recent research has continued to alter such assumptions and largely debunked this landlubber misimpression of the Mongols as vaunted horsemen but haplessly inept sailors. Moreover, the scholarship that has ensued from it reveals just how thoroughly these conquerors engaged in exploiting the surrounding seas, often through the ingenuity and with the assistance of non-Mongols, for the purpose of maximizing every advantage, especially whenever and wherever it had any bearing on trade (May, 2012: 125–28). Indeed, we in fact learn from these studies, such as the highly revealing book on

---

[41] Duyvendak wrote Zanj as "Zanggi."

Muslim merchant activity in China under the Mongols by historian John Chaffee, that, along with that for incense, aromatics, spices, perfumes, ivory, and rhinoceros horn, the Chinese demand especially for slaves remained as robust as ever (Chaffee, 2018: 133).

Instead, our dearth in knowledge about the Zanj of Yuan times who might have entered China by sea is probably better explained less by the exaggeration of Mongol seafaring incompetence than by two other factors. First, under Mongol dominion, there was simply a much-improved viability for Zanj, whether free or enslaved, to enter China overland (Roux, 2002 [repr. 2003]: 66, 92). Second, in the unprecedentedly multicultural environment fostered especially under the emperor Khubilai Khan, during his reign from 1260 to 1294, the presence of Africans within the coterie of foreigners ensconced at the imperial court may well have been so commonplace as to be undeserving of comment (Roux, 2002 [repr. 2003]: 92; Wyatt, 2017: 306–11).

To be sure, the overall trend toward increased accuracy in the cultural description of the world that was initiated during the last century of the Song period aligned especially well with and was methodically perpetuated by Mongol self-interests. This tendency became quite valuably exerted in and reflected by the discipline of cartography (Lo, 2012: 108). To our great fortune, one of the best surviving examples of this tendency exists in the form of an off-center depiction of the southernmost tip of Africa by the notable geographer Zhu Siben 朱思本 (1273–1337); it is thought to have been drawn in the early fourteenth century, between the years 1311 and 1320 (Wilkinson, 1973 [repr. 2015]: 205, 397; Snow, 1988 [repr. 1989]: 9, 10). Considering that the map was produced by an individual who had never visited the site he drew and who had only secondhand information to arrive at a representation, the rendering is stunningly accurate in that the location it is meant to convey is so immediately recognizable to us in the modern day (Filesi, 1972: 25, 79). Furthermore, upon even closer inspection, perhaps on account of the singularity of its placement, an offshore island – just to the east of but still contiguous with the main shoreline of the continent – captures our attention as the only other major discrete element in the composition of the map. Its positioning indeed marks it as a site corresponding very closely to what was then and is now Zanzibar (Filesi, 1972: 41, 42, 45, 46, 71, 78). Amidst the profusion of inconspicuous labeling, this island is strikingly and discernibly demarcated not as a place but as a people. In Chinese, *sangce* 桑册 is an otherwise meaningless phoneme meant almost surely as yet another attempt at approximating *zanj* or "black" (Dathorne, 1996: 81, 98–100, 117; Wilensky, 2002: 33); *nu* 奴, best interpreted in the plural in this context, can have no meaning other than "slaves." (See Figure 5)

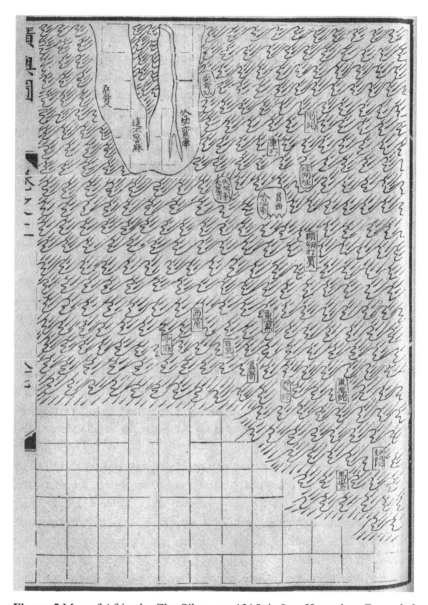

Figure 5 Map of Africa by Zhu Siben, ca. 1315, in Luo Hongxian, *Expanded Edition of Imperial Maps*, 1555.

The fall of the Yuan dynasty and the expulsion of the Mongols as conquerors gave rise to the establishment of the Ming dynasty. Generally assessed by representing the return to Chinese rule following the scourge of Mongol domination, the Ming was as incurious about the world at large as the Yuan had been curious. Over its entire duration, only one consequential event of the Ming militated against this broadly exclusionary outlook, and it was the famed series of maritime voyages across and throughout the Indian Ocean embarked on and successfully completed under the command of the imperial eunuch admiral Zheng He 鄭和 (1371–1435) (Wilkinson, 1973 [repr. 2015]: 794–96).

These fabled explorations that Zheng He led all occurred between 1405 and 1433, with each venture averaging in excess of two years of time at sea. We can rightly regard these undertakings as the renowned technical achievements that they were because each involved hundreds of the largest known ships of the age mobilized by tens of thousands in personnel (Dreyer, 2006 [repr. 2007]: 99–134). However, almost invariably overlooked is the fact that – inasmuch as the concept was understood, pursued, and practiced at that time – the flotillas that Zheng He commanded also functioned as vehicles of inter-cultural courtesy. Detachments from Zheng He's massive fleets first made contact with East African shores in the year 1418, midway through the fifth of his seven voyages mainly south and west across the Indian Ocean (Dreyer, 2006 [repr. 2007]: 82–91; Wyatt, 2010: 103). On this mission, the embassy from Malindi – being identical with the modern city in what is now contemporary Kenya – was the principal group of tribute-bearers to China from Africa that Zheng He escorted back to its homeland (Dreyer, 2006 [repr. 2007]: 32, 83, 89, 90). Thus, these seagoing expeditions of the early fifteenth century – before they were abruptly terminated – verged on facilitating new bridges across the cultural chasm separating Africa and China (Dreyer, 2006 [repr. 2007]: 166–71). We must instead regard them now as being among the last best opportunities lost.

With the cessation of the remarkable set of expeditionary voyages undertaken by Zheng He over the course of the first third of the fifteenth century, the trafficking of Africans into China – whether under Chinese or any other auspices – also ceased or, at the very least, slowed to a trickle. Ming seclusion policies led to no substantive flow of Africans into China being resumed for nearly a century (Filesi, 1972: 67). However, when the Chinese were once again exposed to Africans in quantifiable numbers they encountered them as anything but free men and, moreover, these enslaved human imports were in the tow of entirely different masters than in the past. These new masters of the Zanj were the imperialist-minded Europeans and, with the turn of the sixteenth century and yet hardly without confrontation, they succeeded for a short stint at least in displacing the seafaring Arabs, Indians, and possibly Malays as keepers of and dealers in enslaved Africans throughout much of the expanse of the Indian Ocean (Parker, 2010 [repr. 2012]: 88–89, 139; Beachey, 1976b: x).

Foremost within the vanguard of the new European presence in Asia as importers of Africans into the Indian Ocean realm were the Portuguese, who also happened to be the first wave among those that would vie to extract especially commercial profits from their dealings with China. By the close of the fifteenth century, the Portuguese were already leading participants in the Atlantic Ocean slave trade, and they subsequently launched their forays into and throughout the Indian Ocean via their newly emergent outposts along the Malabar Coast (the southwestern coastline) of subcontinental India, which had been reached by the explorer Vasco da Gama (ca. 1460s–1524) in 1498. Thereafter, the primary gateway for the new Portuguese presence and, concomitantly, the revived African one throughout the Western Sea became their appropriated Indian state of Goa – Estado da India ("the state of India") – or, as it became in later times sometimes simply called, Portuguese India (Parker, 2010 [repr. 2012]: 20–26; Sheriff, 2014: 37–41).

From Goa, seeking aggressively to establish a monopoly on trade in the East Indies proper, the Portuguese merchants sailed further eastward toward China and Japan. In so venturing, they were invariantly accompanied by either large or small numbers of African slaves, not exclusively for the purpose of labor but oftentimes – given the proclivity for conditionally arming them – for that of personal defense. Indeed, in all their colonizing enterprises, the Portuguese maintained and often exercised a long-standing, if counterintuitive, tradition of arming slaves (Thornton, 2006: 87; Eaton, 2006: 115–35).

Seemingly as often by shipwreck as by design, the carracks of the Portuguese would end up either aground or in distress off the South China Sea (in Chinese, Nanyang 南洋) coastline, frequently in states of disrepair and with their occupants in dire straits. Once ashore, irrespective of how they had come to be encountered by Chinese authorities, whether indeed intentionally or by accident, these visitors were regarded as unwelcome and so treated. If their ships were deemed sufficiently intact, the intruders would be dealt with brusquely and forced back out to sea. If their ships were ruined, they were usually subjected to indeterminate terms of imprisonment, pending being ransomed, if such ever occurred. Worst of all, if they should in any way object to or resist being manhandled and looted by corrupt Chinese authorities when initially encountered, they were typically killed in the most gruesome of manners on the spot (Brook, 2008 [repr. 2009]: 87–94).

From the time that their vessels sailing from their subjugated Malayan entrepôt of Melaka (formerly Malacca) had first reached the great trading port of Guangzhou 廣州 (also Canton) in 1517, Portuguese relations with China improved only gradually and fitfully. Reports emanating from nearby Melaka describing the unfortunate and unseemly nature of Portuguese rule there tended to heighten Chinese wariness and hinder progress. Locally and more directly, the Chinese found the ill-timed construction of a fort just downstream from Guangzhou by Simão Pires de Andrade (d. 1550s?), the wayward younger brother of the diplomat Fernão Pires de Andrade (d. 1552), who was intent on protecting his own fledgling trade at the expense of all rivals, to be gallingly irksome (Cotterell, 2010: 42). Nor was the situation much at all helped by the fact that Simão Pires de Andrade happened to be one of the first and most brazen Portuguese enslavers of Chinese (Fujitani, 2016: 87). These factors among others led Ming authorities to suspend official relations with the Portuguese in 1521, dismissing their ambassadors from the imperial court at Beijing and expelling their fleet from Guangzhou (Cotterell, 2010: 42; Fujitani, 2016: 87).

Nonetheless, matters improved markedly after the Portuguese – just as they had earlier in India – succeeded in securing a territorial base from which to further their interests and activities. In 1535, owing to the usefulness of the gunnery on board their caravels in eradicating the South China Sea piracy threat, as a concession, these traders were grudgingly granted permission by the Ming state to trade at but not settle in Macau (Chinese, Aomen 澳門) (Appleton, 1951: 8). Despite this prohibition forbidding settlement, by 1640, just over a century after the initial dispensation, Macau was populated by 2,000 Portuguese and, no less significantly, by a cohort of slaves that "number[ed] about five thousand," who were substantially if not all Africans imported from various parts of Africa (Boxer, 1948 [repr. 1960]: 143). Once so appropriated by settlement, Macau of course remained autonomous for nearly five centuries, not reverting to the control of Chinese government until 1999. Thus, history reveals the adroitness with which the much-undesired Portuguese colonists exploited and extended what surely the Ming court had originally intended only to be a transitory arrangement.

Enslaved Africans who accompanied their Portuguese captors to China chiefly at Macau indisputably represented a breed apart, to Chinese as well as to other observers, whether Asian or European, because, as historian Charles R. Boxer was to point out: "The oft-made claim that the Portuguese had no color-bar cannot be substantiated" (Boxer, 1961 [repr. 1969]: 42). Whereas the Portuguese kings generally maintained that religion and not color should serve as the qualifier for full citizenship, with all Asian converts to Christianity being treated as equal to their fellow Portuguese co-religionists in the faith, this policy was neither always clear nor consistent. It was not extended either to the native populations of North or South America or to those of Africa. However, whereas there were legal prohibitions against the enslavement of the former, no such constraints applied in the subjugation into bondage of the latter. Indeed, as Boxer astutely concluded, "The sugar plantations of Brazil, the household labour of the Portuguese settlers in three continents, and even to some extent the defence of their settlements, depended mainly on the strong right arms of their (principally African) slaves" (Boxer, 1961 [repr. 1969]: 43–44).[42]

For their part, the members of Ming Chinese officialdom, in their dealings with their ensconced foreign guests, being wary of both European masters and African slaves, reported persistently on the activities of both. Under these conditions of surveillance, a new term – actually, very likely a quite old epithet in the vernacular – arose and broadly entered the lexicon for the former Kunlun or Zanj who hailed from Africa. The term of choice among the general populace was *heigui* 黑鬼, meaning quite literally "black ghost" or "black demon" (Brook, 2008 [repr. 2009]: 95–98). We should not doubt that this designation was uncommonly pejorative. *Heigui* is also distinctive among the changing names for the African under consideration not merely because it is so late in emerging but because it is the first of the names that has no basis in place. Therefore, ironically, even with enhanced amassed knowledge about Africa as a place in hand and more at their disposal than ever previously, the Chinese of late Ming times evinced an utterly profound and fearful repugnance toward its still-miniscule number of liberty-deprived native inhabitants residing in their midst (See Figure 6).

Yet, despite the rise to prominence of such a term of derision as *heigui* among the masses, we find that an all-too-familiar term for the certifiably African blacks in the service of the Portuguese and other foreigners continued to hold sway with the Chinese literati. Perhaps nowhere is this retention better preserved than in the words of the geographer Wang Shixing 王士性 (1546–98), who – writing in his *Guangzhi yi* 廣志繹 (*Record of Extensive Travels Continued*) – observed while at Macau:

> Moreover, there is a category of being aboard the foreign ships that is named "Kunlun slaves," [the same] that the commoners call "black ghosts," and whose entire bodies are as if coated in lacquer, which ends only with the whiteness of their two eyes. These beings heed only the master who feeds and clothes them, disregarding even the master's kin and friends. Whether they live or die is something that only their master can decree, and if the master orders that they should cut their own throats, then so they will do, with no thought to whether slitting their throats is deserved or not.
>
> The Kunlun by nature brandish blades and are skilled at killing. If the master departs and orders his slave to guard the gate, then whether fire or flood occurs, he will perish before escaping. If someone slightly nudges the door-bar or the latch-bolt to a box wherein valuables are kept, with no deliberation on whether he is a thief or not, the slave then simply kills him. These slaves are also skilled at diving and, by using cords tied around their waists, they enter the waters to fetch things. These slaves are purchased by the

---

[42] For more discussion of the variety of labor to which the Portuguese put their African slaves to work, see Phillips, 1985: 148–49, 158–59.

黑鬼

東夷圖像

十

Figure 6 Anonymous. Black devil. From Cai Ruxian, *Portraits of Eastern Barbarians*, 1586.

head, at a cost of fifty or sixty pieces of gold each.[43] (Wang, 2006: 4.293; Brook, 2008 [repr. 2009]: 96–97, 245)

Much can be extracted from Wang Shixing's vivid description of the Kunlun of his day but most salient for us to grasp no doubt, aside from the new attributions

---

[43] This work, which bears a preface dated 1597, is an expansion of Wang's earlier *Guangyou zhi* 廣遊志 (*Record of Extensive Wanderings*).

of dogged obedience and wanton hyper-aggression, is just how imperceptibly little the Chinese apperception and reception of the truly foreign and even more assuredly African slave in their setting, despite the passage of more than six centuries since Song dynastic times, had really changed.

Reports on the presence and plight of the Kunlun qua Africans in China continue substantively with the change to the Qing dynasty (1644–1911). One of the more starkly sobering revelations of the casual ease that Chinese of that time had already early on achieved in their own trading of blacks of any and every extraction comes to us by way of the Guangzhou-area native and traveler Qu Dajun 屈大均 (1630–96), whose book *Guangdong xinyu* 廣東新語 (*News from Guangdong*), prefaced 1680, records his eyewitness accounts. At one juncture, he states: "Of those that the Yue 粵 merchants purchase to send along to Guangzhou, all are yellow-black or jet-black with deep-set eyes. From the familiarity that comes with long stretches of contact, [these blacks] also become capable of Yue speech" (Qu, 1974: 7.234).[44]

Whatever we are destined to know about the saga of the untold numbers of Africans who, preponderantly as slaves, arduously journeyed from the eastern shores of their native continent to China is likely to remain hopelessly fragmentary and discontinuous. Therefore, even with our acquired knowledge, in the end, we still face a litany of imponderable questions. Yet, in my view, one of these imponderables transcends all the others in importance because being able to answer it satisfactorily would best account for why there was any trafficking of Africans into China at all.

In short and in sum, especially with respect to the first wave of viably African slaves in China – those who would have been subsumed along with others under the variegated rubric of Kunlun and other catchall terms – we must ask ourselves what their collective function was intended to have been. Especially within a civilization that at no stage in its history relied on a slave class or its labor as the dominant mode of production (Manning, 1990: 28), what was the motive purpose for the importation of foreign slaves in general and African slaves in particular? Well, although they are neither disinterested nor dispassionate, we have surely garnered a very palpable sense of how they functioned at least by the stage of the transition from Ming to Qing times via the above most illuminating firsthand eyewitness testimonies of Wang Shixing and Qu Dajun.

Albeit wholly in a discursive and largely impressionistic manner, even the earliest sources are not completely silent on this question. Still, whether we elect to consider the particular Kunlun described therein as ethnically African or otherwise, for the period of the Tang dynasty, the data is

---

[44] Yue is an old simplified, shorthand name for Guangdong province.

disproportionately fictional and thus fanciful (Irwin, 1977: 172–76; Campbell, 2008: 21). Nevertheless, for the Zanj slaves of East Africa that either directly via Persia or the satraps of Arabia or circuitously via South China Sea states like Java began to appear toward the end of Tang and beginning of Song times, we may have a still speculative but not completely opaque picture. We can observe that neither in the lands under Islamic dominion nor in China for the contemporaneous era were slaves at any point the main basis of production, as they had been, for example, in the earlier Roman Empire. Referring specifically to the epoch when the caliphate of the Abbāsids was at its greatest territorial extent in about the year 850, the historian Bernard Lewis observed that whereas they were mainly utilized domestically and militarily (especially, in the latter instance, in the formulation of the Mamlūk armies), slaves were sometimes exceptionally used for labor in large-scale undertakings in mining, fleet production, and dredging (Lewis, 1950 [repr. 2002]: 112). As we have seen, albeit largely under personal auspices as guardsmen and retainers, the *heigui* or "black ghosts" functioned quite similarly in Ming China under their Portuguese masters.

Although we cannot know conclusively whether it was equally exceptional, Chinese sources of ensuing Song, Yuan, Ming, and early Qing dynastic times indicate that those Africans entering China who were misfortunate enough not to be gifted as tribute were subjected to a fate very similar to their brethren held in Arab, Mongol, or Portuguese captivity. Again, the uncharacteristically revealing observations of Wang Shixing and especially Qu Dajun only reinforce this conclusion. We learn from the otherwise extremely sparse but still surviving records that the labor of these slaves was expended in numerous capacities. Especially during the eras immediately leading to fullest documentation in the sixteenth century, the descriptions that these extant texts purvey to us portray the Kunlun – perhaps already becoming incrementally more African than Malay – toiling for their Chinese masters as stevedores, divers, and menders of the hulls of damaged or grounded ships (Irwin, 1977: 168–71; Campbell, 2008: 21). Neither to be overlooked nor discounted is how much the reported facility of many of the Kunlun – especially at these seaward labors with which they were tasked – reinforces the likelihood of their origins in one or another now indeterminable marine society. No small number of these African Kunlun were surely forced to live out their bonded lives, laboring from dawn to dusk, either on or near the very waters across which they had been distantly ferried into slavery in China.

This critical question of the precise function of African slaves within traditional Chinese society is complicated all the more by the fact that China had from prehistoric until fairly recent times practiced and condoned *endogenous* slavery, whereby Chinese have for generation upon generation enslaved other Chinese. Being mindful of the limited contribution of slavery historically to economic production in China overall, we must unavoidably ponder what factor or factors must have driven the demand for the *exogenous* slave. Given the limited reliance on their labor, would not the native slaves have served as well as any foreign ones? Assuming the exploitation of native versus non-native slave labor at most times to have been close to if exactly equal in efficiency, what then would have been the compelling need for the introduction of African slaves?

Ultimately, however, our progressing toward an answer to the question of the purpose served by the African slave in China might well be impeded by one of the very presumptions on which it is premised – namely, the presupposition that there *was* in fact strictly from the Chinese perspective any such real need. Recognizing the ever-widening gulf of time between those earliest Africans to enter China and ourselves, we can never fully reject the prospect that – for those Chinese who could afford to procure them – they represented hardly more than objects of exotica. Might they not have been simply curios obtained to help satiate an overpowering fetish for possessing the unusual? To acknowledge this possibility, on the one hand, risks trivializing the tragically unrecoverable experiences of these long-departed slaves. However, on the other hand, not to acknowledge it results only in the willfully irresponsible avoidance of the potential truth.

An East Asian Mode of Medieval Slavery?

Given the vantage point that we now occupy in our understanding of the workings of the various systems of slavery that were operative in East Asia during its Middle Ages, perhaps we can reasonably and appropriately ponder and posit whether there were any singularly integrative threads. After all, inasmuch as we are inclined even to think of medieval East Asia as already constituting a coherent geo-unit, we should also expect to find that there were social infrastructures, extending even to an institution like slavery, that under-laid and underpinned that coherence. Indeed, was there in fact, in its medieval guise, any normative East Asian mode of slavery? In venturing an answer, owing to its preeminent cultural stature, in the pattern that has become estab-lished but for the final time, let us turn first to China.

If we return to reflect even momentarily on the opening initial description of what we can archaeologically reconstruct of the situation in ancient China, one really does struggle to make the argument that the genesis of slavery was predicated on anything other than warfare. As I hope has been persuasively shown, the fact that slavery was premised most either by war or by similarly violent activity involving battle, such as acts of rebellion by those within or resistance by those outside the dominating culture, was to remain an operational constant. Such has been illustrated above particularly through a case study as representative as the Jingkang Incident but also otherwise, leading us to reasonably conclude that, in China, war assuredly remained the prime impetus behind slavery throughout premodern history, up to and throughout most, if not all, of the medieval age.

What can we say of medieval Korea, Japan, and Vietnam? In truth, in all three cases, during medieval times, the very same dynamic, in which slavery was spawned most consistently by war, was at work. Regarding Korea, as Ellen Salem remarks early on in her insightful dissertation study, during the tribal period that preceded the first establishment of a unified kingdom under the Goryeo dynasty in the seventh century, "the large number of slaves held by the Puyŏ [Buyeo] and Koguryŏ [Goguryeo] resulted from their adherence to the practice of enslaving prisoners of war.[45] Penal enslavement was also a feature of these societies, but it alone could not account for the large number of slaves the Chinese chronicles reported them possessing" (Salem, 1978: 34). Reinforcing Salem's observations, Eugene Park notes that in Baekje as well as in Goguryeo, up until the fourth century, a formal assembly of lower-ranking courtiers "functioned as an aristocratic council that deliberated on serious crimes, sentencing criminals to death and turning family members into slaves" (Park, 2022: 36). As Wayne Farris has observed, Japan also presents us with a case in which slavery was most incipiently precipitated and perpetuated by war (Farris, 2009b: 26). He states that, from about 600 CE until as late as the sixteenth century, "The commoner class grew in both size and specialization, and the wars produced more slaves and outcasts than ever before" (Farris, 2009b: 182). Remarking further on the Japanese even on the threshold of unification at the turn of the seventeenth century, he adds that, "As a result of the wars and famines, more people fell victim to servitude all over Japan" (Farris, 2009b: 188). In the case of Vietnam, of citable authorities, the incisive claim of Dang Trinh Ky possibly remains simultaneously the most sweeping but also the most context-rendering because, as he tendered, "In Annam, as elsewhere, the first provider of slaves must have been war" (Dang, 1933: 8).

Whereas it was intended delineate the origin of slaving practice in ancient Vietnam, Dang Trinh Ky's assertion obviously is richly laden with implications that extend well beyond any particular place or time. War as the wellspring and

---

[45] The state of Buyeo 부여 (Chinese, Fuyu 扶餘), founded sometime in the late second century BCE, was centered on modern-day northern Manchuria. Effectively destroyed by the second of two Xianbei invasions in CE 346, its remnants were eventually annexed by Goguryeo in 494.

mainspring of slavery, bondage, and human trafficking is unique neither to East Asia nor to the medieval period of history. Yet the fact that a mode of institutionalized subjugation might even have been globally shared and subscribed to hardly diminishes its overarching and overbearing significance as the presumptive operational enslavement framework that was so perniciously imposed on untold numbers of individuals across the medieval East Asian world, who had no defense against it. To regard it as anything less underestimates the enormities of its debilitating scope and depth. Devaluing its singularity results only in disservice to the legacies of the countless medieval East Asian minions whose lives, liberties, and aspirations, oftentimes from birth, were so summarily oppressed and unforgivingly crushed by it.

References

Abramson, Marc S. (2008). *Ethnic Identity in Tang China*. Philadelphia: University of Pennsylvania Press.

Appleton, William W. (1951). *A Cycle of Cathay: The Chinese Vogue in England during the Seventeenth and Eighteenth Centuries*. New York: Columbia University Press.

Asakawa, Kan'ichi. (1963). *The Early Institutional Life of Japan: A Study in the Reform of 645 A.D.* 1903; repr., New York: Paragon Book Reprint Corporation.

Beachey, R. W. (1976a). *The Slave Trade of Eastern Africa*. London: Rex Collings.

Beachey, R. W. (1976b). *A Collection of Documents on the Slave Trade of Eastern Africa*. London: Rex Collings.

Beckwith, Christopher I. (2011). *Empires of the Silk Road: A History of Central Eurasia from the Bronze Age to the Present*. 2009; repr., Princeton, NJ: Princeton University Press.

Benn, Charles. (2002). *China's Golden Age: Everyday Life in the Tang Dynasty*. Oxford: Oxford University Press.

Biran, Michal. (2021). "Forced Migrations and Slavery in the Mongol Empire (1206–1368)," in *The Cambridge World History of Slavery, Volume 2: AD 500–AD 1420*, eds. Craig Perry, David Eltis, Stanley L. Engerman, and David Richardson. Cambridge: Cambridge University Press.

Bossler, Beverly. (2012). *Courtesans, Concubines, and the Cult of Female Fidelity: Gender and Social Change in China, 1000–1400*. Cambridge, MA: Harvard University Asia Center, Harvard University Press.

Boxer, C. R. (1960). *Fidalgos in the Far East, 1550–1770: Fact and Fancy in the History of Macao*. 1948; repr., The Hague: Martinus Nijhoff.

Boxer, C. R. (1969). *Four Centuries of Portuguese Expansion, 1415–1825: A Succinct Survey*. 1961; repr., Berkeley: University of California Press/ Witwatersrand University Press.

Brook, Timothy. (2009). *Vermeer's Hat: The Seventeenth Century and the Dawn of the Global World*. 2008; repr., New York: Bloomsbury Press.

Brown, Delmer M. (1993). "Introduction," in *The Cambridge History of Japan, Volume 1: Ancient Japan*, ed. Delmer M. Brown. Cambridge: Cambridge University Press .

Campbell, Gwyn. (2008). "Slave Trades and the Indian Ocean World," in *India in Africa, Africa in India: Indian Ocean Cosmopolitanisms*, ed. John C. Hawley. Bloomington: Indiana University Press.

Chaffee, John W. (2018). *The Muslim Merchants of Premodern China: The History of a Maritime Asian Trade Diaspora, 750–1400*. Cambridge: Cambridge University Press.

Chen Shou 陳壽. (1984). *Sanguo zhi xuanzhu* 三國志選注 [Selections from Record of the Three Kingdoms], ed. Miao Yue 繆鉞. Beijing: Zhonghua shuju/Xinhua shudian Beijing faxingsuo faxing.

Cotterell, Arthur. (2010). *Western Power in Asia: Its Slow Rise and Swift Fall, 1415–1999*. Singapore: John Wiley & Sons.

Dang Trinh Ky. (1933). *Le nantissement des personnes dans l'ancien droit annamite* [The pledge of people in the ancient Annamese law]. Paris: Domat-Montchrestien.

Dathorne, O. R. (1996). *Asian Voyages: Two Thousand Years of Constructing the Other*. Westport, CT: Bergen & Garvey.

Davis, Richard L. (1996). *Wind Against the Mountain: The Crisis of Politics and Culture in Thirteenth-Century China*. Cambridge, MA: Council on East Asian Studies, Harvard University.

Dawson, Raymond. (1972). *Imperial China*. London: Hutchinson & Co., Ltd.

Delgado, James P. (2008). *Khubilai Khan's Lost Fleet: In Search of a Legendary Armada*. Berkeley: University of California Press.

Dikötter, Frank. (2015). *The Discourse of Race in Modern China*. 1992; repr., Oxford: Oxford University Press.

Dreyer, Edward L. (2007). *Zheng He: China and the Oceans in the Early Ming Dynasty, 1405–1433*. 2006; repr., New York: Longman.

Duan Chengshi 段成式. (1975). *Youyang zazu* 酉陽雜俎 [Miscellany of Tidbits from Youyang Mountain Cave]. Taipei: Taiwan xuesheng shuju.

Duyvendak, J. J. L. (1949). *China's Discovery of Africa: Lectures Given at the University of London on January 22 and 23, 1947*. London: Arthur Probsthain.

Eaton, Richard M. (2006). "The Rise and Fall of Military Slavery in the Deccan, 1450–1650," in *Slavery and South Asian History*, eds. Indrani Chatterjee and Richard M. Eaton. Bloomington: Indiana University Press.

Ebrey, Patricia Buckley. (2003). *Women and the Family in Chinese History*. 2002; repr., London: Routledge.

Ebrey, Patricia Buckley. (2006). "Introduction," in *Emperor Huizong and Late Northern Song China: The Politics of Culture and the Culture of Politics*, eds. Patricia Buckley Ebrey and Maggie Bickford. Cambridge, MA: Harvard University Asia Center, Harvard University Press.

Ebrey, Patricia Buckley. (2014). *Emperor Huizong*. Cambridge, MA: Harvard University Press.

Elliott, Mark C. (2001). *The Manchu Way: The Eight Banners and Ethnic Identity in Late Imperial China*. Stanford: Stanford University Press.

Farris, William Wayne. (2009a). *Daily Life and Demographics in Ancient Japan*. Ann Arbor: Center for Japanese Studies, University of Michigan.

Farris, William Wayne. (2009b). *Japan to 1600: A Social and Economic History*. Honolulu: University of Hawai'i Press.

Filesi, Teobaldo. (1972). *China and Africa in the Middle Ages*, tr. David L. Morison. London: Frank Cass, Central Asian Research Centre.

Franke, Herbert. (1994). "The Chin Dynasty," in *The Cambridge History of China, Volume 6: Alien Regimes and Border States, 710–1368*, eds. Herbert Franke and Denis C. Twitchett. Cambridge: Cambridge University Press.

Fujitani, James. (2016). "The Ming Rejection of the Portuguese Embassy of 1517: A Reassessment," *Journal of World History* 27.1: 87–102.

Goodrich, L. Carrington. (1931). "Negroes in China," *Bulletin of the Catholic University of Peking* 8: 137–39.

Goodwin, Jennifer R. (2007). *Selling Songs and Smiles: The Sex Trade in Heian and Kamakura Japan*. Honolulu: University of Hawai'i Press.

Hall, John Whitney. (1966). *Government and Local Power in Japan, 500 to 1700: A Study Based on Bizen Province*. Princeton, NJ: Princeton University Press.

Hane, Mikiso. (1991). *Premodern Japan: A Historical Survey*. Boulder, CO: Westview Press.

Hansen, Valerie. (1995). *Negotiating Daily Life in Traditional China: How Ordinary People Used Contracts, 600–1400*. New Haven, CT: Yale University Press.

Hansen, Valerie. (2015). *The Open Empire: A History of China to 1800*, 2nd ed. New York: W. W. Norton & Company.

Hao Jing 郝經. (1983). *Lingchuan ji* 陵川集 [Ling River Collection]. Taipei: Taiwan shangwu yinshuguan [Taiwan Commercial Press].

Harris, Joseph E. (1971). *The African Presence in Asia: Consequences of the East African Slave Trade*. Evanston, IL: Northwestern University Press.

Henthorn, William E. (1974). *A History of Korea*. 1971; repr., New York: Free Press.

Hirth, Friedrich. (1909). "Early Chinese Notices of East African Territories," *Journal of the American Oriental Society* 30.1: 46–57.

Holcombe, Charles. (2011). *A History of East Asia: From the Origins of Civilization to the Twenty-First Century*. Cambridge: Cambridge University Press.

Hookham, Hilda. (1970). *A Short History of China*. New York: St. Martin's Press.

Irwin, Graham W. (1977). *Africans Abroad: A Documentary History of the Black Diaspora in Asia, Latin America, and the Caribbean During the Age of Slavery*. New York: Columbia University Press.

Jackson, Peter. (2017). *The Mongols and the Islamic World: From Conquest to Conversion*. New Haven, CT: Yale University Press.

Johnson, Wallace, tr. (1979). *The T'ang Code*. Princeton, NJ: Princeton University Press.

Kang, David C. (2012). *East Asia Before the West: Five Centuries of Trade and Tribute*. 2010; repr., New York: Columbia University Press.

Kiernan, Ben. (2019). *Việt Nam: A History from Earliest Times to the Present*. 2017; repr., New York: Oxford University Press.

Kiley, Cornelius J. (1999). "Provincial Administration and Land Tenure in Early Heian," in *The Cambridge History of Japan, Volume 2: Heian Japan*, eds. Donald H. Shively and William H. McCullough. Cambridge: Cambridge University Press.

Kim, Bok Rae. (2004). "*Nobi*: A Korean System of Slavery," in *The Structure of Slavery in Indian Ocean Africa and Asia*, ed. Gwyn Campbell. London: Frank Cass Publishers.

Kim, Bok-Rae. (2009). "The Third Gender," in *Children in Slavery through the Ages*, eds. Gwyn Campbell, Suzanne Miers, and Joseph C. Miller. Athens: Ohio University Press.

Kye, Seung B. (2021). "Slavery in Medieval Korea," in *The Cambridge World History of Slavery, Volume 2: AD 500–AD 1420*, eds. Craig Perry, David Eltis, Stanley L. Engerman, and David Richardson. Cambridge: Cambridge University Press.

Lai, Guolong. (2015). *Excavating the Afterlife: The Archaeology of Early Chinese Religion*. Seattle: University of Washington Press.

Leur, J. C. van. (1967). *Indonesian Trade and Society: Essays in Asian Social and Economic History*, 2nd ed. 1955; repr., The Hague: W. van Hoeve.

Levine, Ari Daniel. (2009). "The Reigns of Hui-tsung (1100–1126) and Ch'in-tsung (1126–1127) and the Fall of the Northern Sung," in *The Cambridge History of China, Volume 5, Part I: The Sung Dynasty and Its Precursors, 907–1279*, eds. Paul Jakov Smith and Denis C. Twitchett. Cambridge: Cambridge University Press.

Lewis, Bernard. (2002). *The Arabs in History*. 1950; repr., Oxford: Oxford University Press.

Lewis, Mark Edward. (2009). *China's Cosmopolitan Empire: The Tang Dynasty*. Cambridge, MA: Belknap Press of Harvard University Press.

Li Tana. (2006). "A View from the Sea: Perspectives on the Northern and Central Vietnamese Coast," *Journal of Southeast Asian Studies* 37.1: 83–102.

Lo Jung-pang. (2012). *China as a Sea Power 1127–1368: A Preliminary Survey of the Maritime Expansion and Naval Exploits of the Chinese People During the Southern Song and Yuan Periods*, ed. Bruce A. Elleman. Hong Kong: University of Hong Kong Press and National University of Singapore Press.

Loewe, Michael. (2005). *Everyday Life in Early Imperial China: During the Han Period, 202 BC–AD 220*. 1968; repr., Indianapolis, IN: Hackett Publishing Company, Inc.

Lorge, Peter. (2005). *War, Politics and Society in Early Modern China, 900–1795*. London: Routledge.

Lovins, Christopher. (2022). "Korea: A Slave Society," in *Slavery and Bonded Labor in Asia, 1250–1900*, ed. Richard B. Allen. Leiden: Brill.

Major, John S. and Constance C. Cook. (2017). *Ancient China: A History*. London: Routledge.

Maki Hidemasa 牧英正. (1971). *Jinshin baibai* 人身売買 [The Buying and Selling of Human Bodies]. Tokyo: Iwanami shoten.

Manning, Patrick. (1990). *Slavery and African Life: Occidental, Oriental, and African Slave Trades*. Cambridge: Cambridge University Press.

May, Timothy. (2012). *The Mongol Conquests in World History*. London: Reaktion Books.

McCullough, William H. (1999a). "The Heian Court, 794–1070," in *The Cambridge History of Japan, Volume 2: Heian Japan*, eds. Donald H. Shively and William H. McCullough. Cambridge: Cambridge University Press.

McCullough, William H. (1999b). "The Capital and Its Society," in *The Cambridge History of Japan, Volume 2: Heian Japan*, eds. Donald H. Shively and William H. McCullough. Cambridge: Cambridge University Press.

McNaughton, William. (1971). *The Book of Songs*. New York: Twayne.

Miers, Suzanne. (2004). "Slavery: A Question of Definition," in *The Structure of Slavery in Indian Ocean Africa and Asia*, ed. Gwyn Campbell. London: Frank Cass Publishers.

Mitamura, Taisuke. (1992). *Chinese Eunuchs: The Structure of Intimate Politics*, tr. Charles A. Pomeroy. 1970; repr., Rutland, VT: Charles E. Tuttle Company.

Mote, F. W. (1999). *Imperial China, 900–1800*. Cambridge, MA: Harvard University Press.

Murphey, Rhoads. (1997). *East Asia: A New History*. 1996; repr., New York: Longman.

Nai'an 耐庵, comp. (1994[?]). *Jingkang baishi qizhong* 靖康稗史七种 [Seven Accounts of Jingkang]. *Congshu jicheng xubian* 叢書集成續編 ed. Shanghai: Shanghai shudian.

Ouyang Xiu 歐陽修, Song Qi 宋祁 et al. (1976). *Xin Tangshu* 新唐書 [New History of the Tang]. Taipei: Dingwen shuju.

Palais, James B. (1996). *Confucian Statecraft and Korean Institutions: Yu Hyŏngwŏn and the Late Chosŏn Dynasty.* Seattle: University of Washington Press.

Palais, James B. (1998). *Views on Korean Social History.* Seoul: Institute for Modern Korean Studies, Yonsei University.

Park, Eugene Y. (2022). *Korea: A History.* Stanford: Stanford University Press.

Parker, Charles H. (2012). *Global Interactions in the Early Modern* Age, *1400–1800.* 2010; repr., Cambridge: Cambridge University Press.

Patterson, Orlando. (1982). *Slavery and Social Death: A Comparative Study.* Cambridge, MA: Harvard University Press.

Phillips, Jr., William D. (1985). *Slavery from Roman Times to the Early Transatlantic Trade.* Minneapolis: University of Minnesota Press.

Pratt, Keith. (2006). *Everlasting Flower: A History of Korea.* London: Reaktion Books.

Pulleyblank, E. G. (1958). "The Origins and Nature of Chattel Slavery in China," *Journal of Economic and Social History of the Orient* 1.2: 185–220.

Qu Dajun 屈大均. (1974). *Guangdong xinyu* 廣東新語 [News from Guangdong]. [Jiulong]: Zhonghua shuju.

Rizō, Takeuchi. (1999). "The Rise of the Warriors," in *The Cambridge History of Japan, Volume 2: Heian Japan*, eds. Donald H. Shively and William H. McCullough. Cambridge: Cambridge University Press.

Rodriguez, Junius R. (1999). *Chronology of World Slavery.* Santa Barbara, CA: ABC-CLIO, Inc.

Roux, Jean-Paul. (2003). *Genghis Khan and the Mongol Empire*, tr. Toula Ballas. 2002; repr., New York: Harry N. Abrams.

Ruch, Barbara. (1997). "The Other Side of Culture in Medieval Japan," *in The Cambridge History of Japan, Volume 3: Medieval Japan*, ed. Kozo Yamamura. 1990; repr., Cambridge: Cambridge University Press.

Salem, Ellen. (1978). "Slavery in Medieval Korea," Columbia University Ph.D. dissertation.

Salem Unruh, Ellen. (1976). "The Landowning Slave: A Korean Phenomenon," *Korea Journal* 16.4: 31.

Sansom, G. B. (1962). *Japan: A Short Cultural History.* 1931; repr., London: The Cresset Press.

Sansom, George. (1958). *A History of Japan to 1334, Volume 1.* Stanford: Stanford University Press.

Schafer, Edward H. (1963). *The Golden Peaches of Samarkand: A Study of T'ang Exotics.* Berkeley: University of California Press.

Schafer, Edward H. (1967). *The Vermillion Bird: T'ang Images of the South.* Berkeley: University of California Press.

Schrenck, Leopold von. (1858). *Reisen und Forschungen im Amur-Lande in den Jahren 1854–1856, im Auftrage der Kaiserl* [Travel and Research in the Amur Country in the Years 1854–1856, on Behalf of the Kaiserl]. St. Petersburg: Kaiserliche Akademie der Wissenschaften.

Seth, Michael J. (2016). *A Concise History of Korea: From Antiquity to the Present*, 2nd ed. Lanham, MD: Rowman & Littlefield.

Sheriff, Abdul. (2014). "Globalisation with a Difference: An Overview," in *The Indian Ocean: Oceanic Connections and the Creation of New Societies*, ed. Abdul Sheriff and Engseng Ho. London: C. Hurst & Co.

Shin, Leo K. (2007). "Ming China and Its Border with Annam," in *The Chinese State at the Borders*, ed. Diana Lary. Vancouver: University of British Columbia Press.

Snow, Philip. (1989). *The Star Raft: China's Encounter with Africa*. 1988; repr., Ithaca, NY: Cornell University Press.

Standen, Naomi. (2007). *Unbounded Loyalty: Frontier Crossing in Liao China*. Honolulu: University of Hawai'i Press.

Tao, Jing-shen. (1977). *The Jurchen in Twelfth-Century China: A Study of Sinicization*. Seattle: University of Washington Press.

Taylor, Keith Weller. (1983). *The Birth of Vietnam*. Berkeley: University of California Press.

Taylor, K. W. (2013). *A History of the Vietnamese*. Cambridge: Cambridge University Press.

Thornton, John. (2006). "Armed Slaves and Political Authority in Africa in the Era of the Slave Trade, 1450–1800," in *Arming Slaves: From Classical Times to the Modern Age*, eds. Christopher Leslie Brown and Philip D. Morgan. New Haven. CT: Yale University Press.

Toshiya, Torao. (1993). "Nara Economic and Social Institutions," tr. William Wayne Farris, in *The Cambridge History of Japan, Volume 1: Ancient Japan*, ed. Delmer M. Brown. Cambridge: Cambridge University Press.

Tran, Nhung Tuyet. (2018). *Familial Properties: Gender, State, and Society in Early Modern Vietnam, 1463–1778*. Honolulu: University of Hawai'i Press.

Tuotuo 脱脱 et al. (1977). *Songshi* 宋史 [Song History]. Beijing: Zhonghua shuju.

Wang Shixing 王士性. (2006). *Guangzhi yi* 廣志繹 [Record of Extensive Travels Continued]. Beijing: Zhonghua shuju.

Wang, Xi. (1998). "China," in *Macmillan Encyclopedia of World Slavery, Volume 1 (A–K)*, eds. Paul Finkelman and Joseph C. Miller. New York: Macmillan Reference USA, Simon & Schuster Macmillan.

Wang Yi-t'ung. (1953). "Slaves and Other Comparable Social Groups during the Northern Dynasties (386–618)," *Harvard Journal of Asiatic Studies* 16.3/4: 293–364.

Weinstein, Stanley. (1999). "Aristocratic Buddhism," in *The Cambridge History of Japan, Volume 2: Heian Japan*, eds. Donald H. Shively and William H. McCullough. Cambridge: Cambridge University Press.

Whitmore, John K. (1984). "Social Organization and Confucian Thought in Vietnam," *Journal of Southeast Asian Studies* 15.2: 296–306.

Wilbur, C. Martin. (2016). *Slavery in China during the Former Han Dynasty, 206 B.C.–A.D. 25*. Chicago: Field Museum of Natural History, 1943; repr., Delhi: Facsimile Publishers.

Wilensky, Julie. (2002). "The Magical *Kunlun* and 'Devil Slaves': Chinese Perceptions of Dark-Skinned People and Africa before 1500," *Sino-Platonic Papers* 122: 1–51.

Wilkinson, Endymion. (2015). *Chinese History: A New Manual*, 4th ed. 1973; repr., Cambridge, MA: Harvard University Asia Center.

Wittfogel, Karl A. and Fêng Chia-shêng. (1949). *History of Chinese Society: Liao, 907–1125*. Philadelphia: American Philosophical Society, Macmillan Co.

Wyatt, Don J. (2010). *The Blacks of Premodern China*. Philadelphia: University of Pennsylvania Press.

Wyatt, Don J. (2014). "A Certain Whiteness of Being: Chinese Perceptions of Self by the Beginning of European Contact," in *Race and Racism in Modern East Asia: Western and Eastern Constructions*, eds. Rotem Kowner and Walter Demel. 2013; repr., Leiden: Brill.

Wyatt, Don J. (2017). "The Image of the Black in Chinese Art," in *The Image of the Black in African and Asian Art*, eds. David Bindman, Suzanne Preston Blier, and Henry Louis Gates, Jr. with Karen C. C. Dalton. Cambridge, MA: Belknap Press of Harvard University Press/Hutchins Center for African and African American Research.

Wyatt, Don J. (2019). "Cargoes Human and Otherwise: Chinese Commerce in East African Goods During the Middle Period," in *Early Global Interconnectivity Across the Indian Ocean World, Volume 1: Commercial Structures and Exchanges*, ed. Angela Schottenhammer. New York: Palgrave Macmillan.

Wyatt, Don J. (2021). "Slavery in Medieval China," in *The Cambridge World History of Slavery, Volume 2: AD 500–AD 1420*, eds. Craig Perry, David Eltis, Stanley L. Engerman, and David Richardson. Cambridge: Cambridge University Press.

Wyatt, Don J. (2022). "Slavery and the Mongol Empire," in *Slavery and Bonded Labor in Asia, 1250–1900*, ed. Richard B. Allen. Leiden: Brill.

Yang, Shao-yun. (2022). *Early Tang China and the World, 618–750 CE*. Cambridge: Cambridge University Press.

Yates, Robin D. S. (2013). "Human Sacrifice and the Rituals of War in Early China," in *Sacrifices humains: Perspectives croisées et representations/Human Sacrifice: Cross-Cultural Perspectives and Representations*, eds. Pierre Bonnechere and Renaud Gagné. Liège, Belgium: Presses Universitaires de Liège.

Ye Ziqi 葉子奇. (1959). *Caomuzi* 草木子 [Master of Grasses and Trees]. Beijing: Zhonghua shuju.

Zhang Tiesheng 張鉄生. (1973). *ZhongFei jiaotongshi chutan* 中非交通史初探 [Preliminary Investigation of the History of Chinese–African Relations], 2nd ed. Beijing: Shenghuo dushu xinzhi sanlian shudian.

Zhao Rugua 趙汝适. (1969). *Zhufan zhi* 諸蕃志 [Description of Foreign Peoples]. Taipei: Guangwen shuju.

Acknowledgments

For the welcome opportunity to address the issue of slavery in its exceedingly underexplored medieval East Asian context in the Element format, I am foremost grateful to series editors Geraldine Heng and Susan Noakes. I also thank the journal editors Elizabeth Casteen and Olivia Holmes for granting permission for the modified reproduction of my article "Sudden Slaves of Avarice: Unfree Women and Warriors of Midimperial China," *Mediaevalia: An Interdisciplinary Journal of Medieval Studies Worldwide* 43: 171–203 (2022), which forms a substantial portion herein of the section "Enslavement by Outsiders in Medieval East Asia: The Jingkang Incident and Aftermath." Finally, I thank two anonymous but critically constructive, positive, and collegial peer reviewers for their genuinely insightful queries, suggestions, correctives, and interventions as well as Athena Wyatt for her deft assistance in helping to procure rights of reproduction for two of the half-dozen uniquely illustrative images that grace this Element.

Cambridge Elements ≡

The Global Middle Ages

Geraldine Heng

University of Texas at Austin

Geraldine Heng is Perceval Professor of English and Comparative Literature at the University of Texas, Austin. She is the author of *The Invention of Race in the European Middle Ages* (2018) and *England and the Jews: How Religion and Violence Created the First Racial State in the West* (2018), both published by Cambridge University Press, as well as *Empire of Magic: Medieval Romance and the Politics of Cultural Fantasy* (2003, Columbia). She is the editor of *Teaching the Global Middle Ages* (2022, MLA), coedits the University of Pennsylvania Press series, RaceB4Race: Critical Studies of the Premodern, and is working on a new book, Early Globalisms: The Interconnected World, 500–1500 CE. Originally from Singapore, Heng is a Fellow of the Medieval Academy of America, a member of the Medievalists of Color, and Founder and Co-director, with Susan Noakes, of the Global Middle Ages Project: www.globalmiddleages.org.

Susan Noakes

University of Minnesota, Twin Cities

Susan Noakes is Professor and Chair of French and Italian at the University of Minnesota, Twin Cities. From 2002 to 2008 she was Director of the Center for Medieval Studies; she has also served as Director of Italian Studies, Director of the Center for Advanced Feminist Studies, and Associate Dean for Faculty in the College of Liberal Arts. Her publications include *The Comparative Perspective on Literature: Essays in Theory and Practice* (co-edited with Clayton Koelb, Cornell, 1988) and *Timely Reading: Between Exegesis and Interpretation* (Cornell, 1988), along with many articles and critical editions in several areas of French, Italian, and neo-Latin Studies. She is the Founder and Co-director, with Geraldine Heng, of the Global Middle Ages Project: www.globalmiddleages.org.

About the Series

Elements in the Global Middle Ages is a series of concise studies that introduce researchers and instructors to an uncentered, interconnected world, c. 500–1500 CE. Individual Elements focus on the globe's geographic zones, its natural and built environments, its cultures, societies, arts, technologies, peoples, ecosystems, and lifeworlds.

Cambridge Elements ☰

The Global Middle Ages

Printed in the United States
by Baker & Taylor Publisher Services